The Morning Meeting Book

Roxann Kriete

STRATEGIES FOR TEACHERS SERIES

All net proceeds from the sale of *The Morning Meeting Book* support the work of Northeast Foundation for Children, Inc., a nonprofit, educational foundation established to demonstrate through teaching, research, and consultation a sensible and systematic approach to schooling.

The stories in this book are all based on real events in the classroom. However, in order to respect the privacy of students, names and many identifying characteristics of students and situations have been changed.

ISBN 1-892989-00-X

Library of Congress catalog card number 98-68612

Third printing September 2000

Photographs: Peter Wrenn, William Elwell, Cherry Wyman, Marlynn K. Clayton

Cover and book design: Woodward Design

NORTHEAST FOUNDATION FOR CHILDREN
71 Montague City Road
Greenfield, MA 01301
1-800-360-6332

www.responsiveclassroom.org

*We would like to thank the Shinnyo-En Foundation for their
generous support of the development of this book.*

*The mission of the Shinnyo-En Foundation is "to bring forth
deeper compassion among humankind, to promote greater harmony,
and to nurture future generations toward building
a more ethical society."*

ACKNOWLEDGMENTS

I want to pay tribute to the co-founders of Northeast Foundation for Children who developed Morning Meeting as it is described in this book. They talked with me, read and critiqued my work, and offered permission to use materials they had created. Most significantly, they trusted me to articulate practices at the core of their life's work. Thank you, *Marlynn, Ruth, Jay,* and *Chip,* for your trust and your encouragement.

I also want to pay tribute to the teachers and students of Greenfield Center School, the lab school for Northeast Foundation for Children, where I first saw Morning Meeting fourteen years ago. Though much has changed, the spirit of curiosity and caring that impressed me then impresses me still. I am grateful for the example and companionship of the Center School community.

While preparing to write this book I visited schools in many towns and cities. In those visits I was inspired over and over by wise and powerful teachers—by their passion for learning and their devotion to the children in their care. I am grateful to the many teachers and students who welcomed me warmly into their classrooms to observe and to participate.

I want to thank: *Mary Beth Forton,* project manager and cherished office mate, for her special blend of keen intelligence and gentle care.

Jay Lord for his conviction that I could and should write this and for shouldering additional work himself to clear my way.

Ruth Charney, for rich and provocative conversations, shared stories, support and suggestions.

Marlynn Clayton, for taking this manuscript to the beach, and for tending so carefully to its detail.

Chip Wood, for many introductions to teachers and schools, and for bringing both his educator's and poet's sensibilities to his reading of this manuscript.

Marian Lubinsky, for countless cups of tea, teaching advice, stories and laughter during the Friday afternoons of my first year of teaching. She taught me much of what I know about the value of collegial conversation.

Sharon Dunn, for the wide-ranging intelligence, wise counsel, and generosity of spirit which have infused her work as a long-time Board member and friend of NEFC.

Bob Strachota, for his constant willingness to examine his own teaching practice, for asking real questions, and for continuing to invite me into the life of his classroom.

Allen Woods, for his editing, done with precision and care.

Jeff and Leslie Woodward, designers, for the care they take with presentation and with people and, Jeff, for his painstaking proofreading.

Jean Truckey for handling so much so capably during this time.

Laurie Euvrard for her enthusiasm for the adventures of learning.

Joan Cenedella for invigorating lunch conversations and for dropping in just when we needed her—and agreeing to stay a while.

Gladys and Bill Jarvis, for cheery Good Mornings, kind and lively interest, and for the roof over our heads.

Libby Woodfin, for documenting activities and gathering information for this project.

Pam Porter for her words of encouragement.

Carol Harford, for her support of and interest in NEFC's work, and for modeling that graciousness and power can walk hand in hand.

Eleanor and Elsie, mothers, whose example reminds me what love, hard work, and courage can achieve.

*I dedicate this book to Russ
and to our children, Ben and Rachel.*

TABLE OF CONTENTS

Just as we know instinctively that it makes sense to identify the most effective practices to teach a subject such as mathematics, take those practices and structure them into a sequenced curriculum, and implement that curriculum with trained professionals during dedicated classroom time, we must recognize now that the same effort must be mustered if we are to succeed in the social and emotional domains. It simply makes sense that if we are to expect children to be knowledgeable, responsible, and caring—and to be so despite significant obstacles—we must teach social and emotional skills, attitudes, and values with the same structure and attention that we devote to traditional subjects.

Maurice Elias et al.
Promoting Social and Emotional Learning:
Guidelines for Educators

"It Mattered that I Came"

AN INTRODUCTION

In the spring of my first year as a secondary school teacher, I got a letter from a student for whom I had a particular fondness, letting me know that she was dropping out of school. School wasn't making much sense to her and little that she was being asked to learn held much interest for her. She wrote, almost apologetically, that school just wasn't a place she felt she belonged. More than twenty years later, her words still seem profoundly sad to me:

I will always remember how you said "Hi, Sue" as I walked into eighth period. It made me feel like it really mattered that I came.

It touched and pained me that something which seemed so small to me, an act I hadn't even been aware of, had meant so much to her. I vowed to learn something from it and became more intentional

All classroom members—grown-ups and students—
gather in a circle at the start of every day for Morning Meeting.

about greeting my students. I stationed myself by the door and tried to say a little something to each one as they entered, or at least to make eye contact and smile at every student, not just the ones like Sue for whom I had an instinctive affinity.

Gradually I realized how much I was learning at my post by the door. I observed who bounced in with head up and smile wide, whose eyes were red-rimmed from tears shed in the girls' room at lunch, who mumbled a response into his collar and averted his eyes every day for an entire semester. I didn't know what to do about much of it, but at least I was learning how to notice.

I have learned a lot since then. It is good for students to be noticed, to be seen by their teacher. But it is only a start, not enough by itself. They must notice and be noticed by each other as well.

Years after I taught Sue, I joined the staff of Greenfield Center School, Northeast Foundation for Children's K–8 lab school. There, I saw teachers teaching students to greet each other, to speak to each other, to listen to each other. I saw students start each day together in Morning Meeting where noticing and being noticed were explicit goals. This book is about Morning Meeting— a particular and deliberate way to begin the school day. Today, many children in kindergartens, elementary and middle schools around the country launch their school days in Morning Meetings.

All classroom members—grown-ups and students—gather in a circle, greet each other, and listen and respond to each others' news. We take note of who is present and who is absent; whether it is still raining or not; who is smiling and buoyant; who is having a hard time smiling. We briefly grapple with problems that challenge our minds and look forward to the events in the day ahead. Morning Meeting allows us to begin each day as a community of caring and respectful learners.

Morning Meeting Format

Morning Meeting is made up of four, sequential components and lasts up to a total of a half hour each day. Although there is much overlap, each component has its own purposes and structure. The components intentionally provide opportunities for children to practice the skills of greeting, listening and responding, group problem-solving, and noticing and anticipating. The daily practice of these four components gradually weaves a web that binds a class together.

1. Greeting: children greet each other by name, often including handshaking, clapping, singing, and other activities.

2. Sharing: students share some news of interest to the class and respond to each other, articulating their thoughts, feelings, and ideas in a positive manner.

3. Group Activity: the whole class does a short activity together, building class cohesion through active participation.

4. News and Announcements: students develop language skills and learn about the events in the day ahead by reading and discussing a daily message posted for them.

Teachers must commit more than just time to implement Morning Meeting. They must also commit themselves to a belief in children's capacity to take care of themselves and each other as they learn social skills like respect and responsibility along with academic skills like vocabulary and algorithms. Morning Meeting creates opportunities for children to practice these social skills. It also creates opportunities for teachers to model these skills and give children valuable feedback. It provides practice in respectful behavior, and helps children stretch the boundaries of their social world.

The time one commits to Morning Meeting is an investment which is repaid many times over. The sense of belonging and the skills of attention, listening, expression and cooperative interaction developed in Morning Meeting are a foundation for every lesson, every transition time, every lining-up, every upset and conflict, all day and all year long. Morning Meeting is a microcosm of the way we wish our schools to be—communities full of learning, safe and respectful and challenging for all.

The Responsive Classroom Approach

The Morning Meeting format described in this book was developed by Northeast Foundation for Children staff as part of an approach to teaching and learning called *The Responsive Classroom®*. It is an approach informed by belief in seven basic tenets.

The Responsive Classroom

1. **The social curriculum is as important as the academic curriculum.**

2. **How children learn is as important as what children learn.**

3. **The greatest cognitive growth occurs through social interaction.**

4. **There is a set of social skills that children need to learn and practice in order to be successful. They form the acronym CARES—Cooperation, Assertion, Responsibility, Empathy, Self-control.**

5. **We must know our children individually, culturally, and developmentally.**

6. All parents want what's best for their children and we must work with parents as partners.

7. The principles of *The Responsive Classroom* must be practiced by educators in their interactions with each other, with the children, and with the parents.

How to Use This Book

You may choose to read the entire book from beginning to end, select sections which immediately grab your attention, or use it as a reference as your Morning Meeting experience grows. The book begins with a fundamental chapter about Morning Meeting as a whole, followed by chapters about each of its four components and a conclusion. The structure is designed to tell three things about Morning Meeting: what it is; why it is; and how to do it.

In the Classroom

Each chapter begins with a section which presents vignettes and documents observations from classrooms during Morning Meetings. Some are from large, urban schools; some are from small, rural schools. Though the demographics vary widely, the spirit and elements of the Morning Meetings are consistent, the children and their teachers familiar to those of us who spend time in schools. These glimpses take you into the middle of classrooms where Morning Meetings are flourishing.

Purposes and Reflections

These articulate the purposes and goals of each component and locate connections to theory and the larger context of learning. They are like a guided tour, highlighting and interpreting some of the powerful moments created in our classrooms and conveying some of the specific details and flavor of well-run Morning Meetings.

Getting Started

These sections offer directions for teachers as they begin to implement the components of Morning Meeting. Directions and examples of teacher language are offered as templates to be used for guidance, not as exact patterns for repetition. Your knowledge of your class's development, pace, needs, and your own teaching style will lead to adaptations that work best for you and your class.

These directions are offered with respect for individual teachers and a wish to empower them. They are offered, also, with the awareness, affirmed by thousands of teachers with whom we have worked, that templates drawn by experienced hands are invaluable tools when starting something new. Feel free to use these templates—trace them, adapt them, refine them—so that they truly serve you. Just keep the purposes and goals of Morning Meeting in mind.

Each section ends with a concise listing of teacher and student responsibilities to help you implement Morning Meeting and assess your practice.

Fine Tunings

These questions and answers address some concerns and issues teachers commonly encounter as their experience with Morning Meeting evolves. This section considers some of the questions teachers frequently ask as they move past the basic introduction of Morning Meeting in their classrooms. These particular questions have surfaced frequently in our own practice and in teaching other teachers over the years.

Morning Meeting

I t's time, it's time, it's time for Morning Meeting now. . ." The melody, begun by the teacher and picked up by the students, drifts down the hall from the kindergarten classroom. Directly upstairs, in a fourth grade room, a student selects the wooden chime from its resting place on a shelf top, and strikes it gently with a mallet. When her classmates quiet down and look at her, she announces simply, "Morning Meeting time." Next door, the teacher of the fifth- and sixth-graders puts his coffee mug on a counter and rings the old-fashioned school bell which is the signal in his room to stop and listen. "Five minute warning. Finish your plans for the day and come to the rug for Morning Meeting."

Teachers and students crave a certain amount of predictability and routine in the school day, especially at the start. The format of Morning Meeting is predictable, but there is plenty of room for variation and change. Meetings reflect the style and flavor of individual teachers and groups. They also reflect the ebb and flow of a school year's seasons—September's new shoes and anxious, careful faces; December's pre-holiday excitement; February's endless runny noses; April's spring-has-sprung exuberance. Its mixture of routine and surprise, of comfort and challenge, make Morning Meeting a treasured and flexible teaching tool.

Purposes and Reflections

The socialization of children has historically been considered an important part of preschools and kindergartens. Learning to play together, to listen to each other, to wait in line are skills that have long been a legitimate part of early childhood curriculum. But Lilian Katz, noted early childhood educator, sees significant benefits for structured interactions beyond the earliest grades: "There is quite a bit to learn from early childhood education experiences that can be 'pushed up' to later grades, instead of the classic pushing down." (Katz 1998, 8)

Preschool and early childhood programs traditionally begin with a ritual, often called Circle Time, which gathers children into a circle for a song, and includes practice in counting skills while taking attendance, and sharing or "Show and Tell" time. Morning Meeting evolved from this accepted practice, building on children's needs for social guidance, structure, and interaction. Morning Meeting is a translation of Circle Time for older students, "pushing up" the goals of socialization and using our detailed knowledge of students' social, emotional and cognitive development.

Educators have learned that social skills are not a checklist to be mastered by the end of kindergarten so that students can get on with the acquisition of academic skills. Instead, social skills are skills we continue to acquire and refine throughout our lives, just like academic skills.

Children need opportunities to practice and define these skills as part of a group at every age. At five, it may be hard to share the box of crayons; at eleven, it is hard to share a friend. At seven, it is a matter of pride to clean the lunchroom table neatly; at thirteen, it is a matter of pride to disdain the same chore. As Dr. Arnold Gesell concluded from his extensive research on child development, growth is not a straight line function. (Ilg et al. 1981) It loops and spirals and zigs and zags, its pattern influenced by characteristics of each person's age, background, and individual temperament.

Teachers have long known and researchers are now confirming that social skills are not just something to be taught so that children behave well enough to get on with the real business of schooling. Rather, they are inextricably intertwined with cognitive growth and intellectual progress. A person who can listen well, who can frame a good question and has the assertiveness to pose it, who can examine a situation from a number of perspectives will be a strong learner. All those skills—skills essential to academic achievement—must be modeled, experienced, practiced, extended and refined in the context of social interaction. Morning Meeting is a forum in which all that happens. It is not an add-on, something extra to make time for, but rather an integral part of the day's planning and curriculum.

Morning Meeting makes important contributions to the tone and content of a classroom. The following broad statements summarize these contributions and each is explored in a section that follows.

Purposes of Morning Meeting

1. **Morning Meeting sets the tone for respectful learning and establishes a climate of trust.**

2. **The tone and climate of Morning Meeting extend beyond the Meeting.**

3. **Morning Meeting motivates children by addressing two human needs: the need to feel a sense of significance and belonging, and the need to have fun.**

4. **The repetition of many ordinary moments of**

respectful interaction in Morning Meeting enables some extraordinary moments.

5. Morning Meeting merges social, emotional, and intellectual learning.

Morning Meeting sets the tone for respectful learning and establishes a climate of trust.

Beginnings can be critical. The leader of a workshop I recently attended asked our group of teachers and principals to recall and describe our first half hour as teachers. A good number of participants were nearing retirement age and their first moments as teachers were more than thirty years ago, but every one of us could recall in vivid detail what happened and how we felt in those first thirty minutes.

Certainly, the first thirty minutes of each day are not as momentous or embedded in memory as the first thirty minutes in a new career. There are some days, in fact, when we can hardly remember at four o'clock in the afternoon what happened at nine o'clock that morning. The details may have flown from our cluttered memory, but it is likely that the pace and flavor of our first half hour in school had a lot to do with the way we felt at four o'clock and whether the day's challenges felt exhilarating or overwhelming. The same is true for our students. Beginnings matter.

The way we begin each day in our classroom sets the tone for learning and speaks volumes about what and whom we value, about our expectations for the way we will treat each other, and about the way we believe learning occurs.

Children's learning begins the second they walk in the doors of the building. Children notice whether they are greeted warmly or overlooked, whether the classroom feels chaotic and unpredictable, or ordered and comforting. If they announce, "My cat got hit by a car last night but it's gonna' be all right," they may find an interested, supportive audience or one that turns away. Every detail of their experience informs students about their classroom and their place in it.

When we start the day with everyone together, face-to-face, welcoming each person, sharing news, listening to individual voices, and communicating as a caring group, we make several powerful statements. We say that every person matters. We say that the way we interact individually and as a group matters. We say that our culture is one of friendliness and thoughtfulness. We say that hard work can be accomplished and important discoveries can be made by playing together. We say that teachers hold authority, even though they are a part of the circle. We say that this is a place where courtesy and warmth and safety reign—a place of respect for all.

In order to learn, we must take risks—offering up a tentative answer we are far from sure is right or trying out a new part in the choir when we are not sure we can hit the notes. We can take these risks only when we know we will be respected and valued, no matter the outcome. We must trust in order to risk, and Morning Meeting helps create a climate of trust.

The tone and climate of Morning Meeting extend beyond the Meeting.

We see this in any number of ways. For instance, children may begin to greet each other spontaneously, even before the Meeting circle has convened. A first grade teacher whose class had been using Morning Meeting for several months wrote: "One Tuesday as I stood by the door, waiting for the class to gather, I just watched. They were genuinely glad to see each other. Some were hugging a greeting. Some were clapping for something. What a joy to watch—I was merely an observer and just loved it."

Sometimes what transfers isn't a specific behavior, such as a greeting, but is instead an attitude. Ruth Charney, author and teacher at the Greenfield Center School, described this scene from the seventh/eighth-grade room she co-taught.

"Time for Meeting," announced the teacher and the students assembled

Morning Meeting helps to create a climate of trust
which encourages children to take risks.

on the low benches arranged around the perimeter of their whole group meeting area. Three students hung back, whispering by the coat rack.

Their teacher addressed them pleasantly: "Daria, Abby, Lindsay, Meeting is starting." The girls exchanged looks and moved toward the circle, pointedly ignoring the space others had made for them, sitting instead on the floor a few feet behind one of the benches. Clearly, they had come into the room with their own agenda.

Their teacher, voice still pleasant but firm, looked straight at them: "You need to move into the circle." They hesitated a moment but then moved as directed.

Quietly, using the structure of the circle, their teacher reminded them of an expectation: You will be fully part of this classroom, not outside of it. Within a few minutes, the three back-benchers were absorbed by a classmate's announcement that a moose had wandered through his back yard that morning.

When Meeting was over, off they went to math groups, chatting with others along the way, their agenda defused, able to be positive participants in classroom life that day.

Morning Meeting motivates children by addressing two human needs: the need to feel a sense of significance and belonging, and the need to have fun.

All of us need to feel that we belong and are valued for the competencies, skills, and knowledge we bring to a group, that our unique contributions are recognized and appreciated. All the components of Morning Meeting speak to those needs directly.

Consulting Teacher Melissa Correa-Connolly of Leominster, Massachusetts, speaks of what she has seen happen, both in her own elementary classroom and in the rooms of many teachers with whom she has worked:

"I think of Morning Meeting as having such immense power because it meets the emotional needs of children. It acknowledges everyone and makes them feel significant. It does away with the feeling many children have of being a piece of furniture in the classroom. Morning Meeting is the first thing in the morning and it allows children to be seen, to have a voice."

Having fun is also a universal human need. Fun is not necessarily synonymous with frivolity or silliness, though it can sometimes be both. It does mean engagement and fascination with what we do. Fun is playful and light-hearted even when the activity is hard and the challenge great. It is not about winning, but about immersion in the pleasure of the activity itself.

Fun might involve striving to find the five punctuation errors planted in the Morning Message or learning to sing "Dona Nobis Pacem" in three-part harmony. It might mean trying to guess the three-digit number a classmate is thinking of in a game called "Pico, Fermé, Nada" *(Appendix E)*. Fun might mean laughing when serious and dignified Amy reports on her new puppy's antics, or it might mean learning a new and lively greeting EJ brought back from summer camp.

Fun is also connected with risk-taking. Risks taken in a playful way can teach us how to handle the more serious risks that growth can demand. The children (and adults) who don't play often have a difficult time reaching their potential because growth almost always requires venturing into the unknown.

One thing is certain. Humans strive to fulfill their needs in whatever way they can, whether those ways are positive or negative. The child who can't be known or recognized in the group for friendly contributions will be known for his trouble-making contributions. And when our programs don't provide ways to meet our students' needs for fun constructively, they will devise their own, often not-so-constructive ways.

Morning Meeting is full of opportunities for a class to have fun together and for all its members to feel a sense of significance and belonging, needs affirmed by theory and research: "Adler (1930) proposed that a sense of belonging motivates children to develop their skills and contribute to the welfare of all. . . . Research indicates that educators who establish firm boundaries, foster warm personal relationships in the classroom, and enable students to have an impact on their environment strengthen students' attachment to their school, their interest in learning, their ability to refrain from self-destructive behaviors, and their positive behaviors." (Elias et al. 1997, 44)

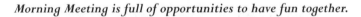

Morning Meeting is full of opportunities to have fun together.

The repetition of many ordinary moments of respectful interaction in Morning Meeting enables some extraordinary moments.

Morning Meeting, repeated every day, is full of moments that by themselves seem quite mundane and ordinary. But this repetition can enable some quite extraordinary accomplishments within and beyond the Meeting circle, too. Consider this story told by a third grade teacher from a school where Morning Meetings were an established part of school life in all the classrooms:

One wintry Tuesday morning at about 9:30, just as Morning Meeting in my room was ending, a second-grader from the classroom adjacent to mine entered and approached me politely. "Excuse me, Mrs. Truesdell, but our teacher isn't here yet. We finished Morning Meeting, but we don't know what to do next."

A series of missed communications including a school secretary with the flu and a faulty answering machine had resulted in a class without a teacher or a substitute. These seven-year-olds knew the routines so well that they had gathered themselves and conducted an orderly and merry Morning Meeting. I remembered, in fact, hearing the strains of the song "River" wafting through the thin wall that connected the two rooms and thinking how much better it sounded than last week!

These children's daily participation in the ongoing routines of Morning Meeting had enabled them to take responsibility for these routines even in the absence of their teacher. Their school celebrated their responsible behavior at an assembly later that week.

The habits of participation established by Morning Meeting routines can also serve a community well in more extreme circumstances. The experience of Joyce Love, a revered elementary school teacher in Washington, D.C., testifies to this.

As a part of Morning Meeting, her class knew how to come quickly together and how to listen respectfully to each other. They had considered hard questions such as "What can you say when someone shares something that's really upsetting to them?" as well as "What might we say when someone shares something that makes them really happy?" They had, under Joyce's guidance, carefully constructed habits of participation, and practiced them day-in and day-out in the most ordinary situations with the most ordinary material—news of a swimming test passed, a baby brother with chicken pox, a visit from relatives.

One morning, several of Joyce's students saw a dead body on a street corner on their walk to school. Now, when they were confronted with an event of monumental impact, they had a familiar circle to come to. They had patterns of sharing and response that helped their teacher to help them begin to deal with a haunting scene. "If it hadn't been for Morning Meeting, I wouldn't have known what to do. Its structures helped take care of things," recalled Joyce.

Not all extraordinary moments enabled by Morning Meeting are tragic, of course. In our K–8 lab school, eighth-graders take a literature course which calls upon them to consider the universal themes of the literary tradition, what educator and author Parker Palmer calls the "big stories" (Palmer 1998), and relate them to the "little stories" of students' own lives, the stories that tell their personal and individual tales.

For the final assignment, each student writes a play based on an event important in his or her life. Students cast and direct these plays, with fellow class members as actors, and present them at Play Night for their families, faculty, and friends. Some plays are light, some somber. One might be elaborately plotted with a dozen characters and several settings; the next might be a minimalist dialogue.

All are presentations by a group of young teens relying on each other to make, in Palmer's language, these "little" stories "big," to make art from what they have witnessed in their lives. It is a profound exercise and everyone does it, not just one gifted group, year after year.

Inspired by attending many years of Play Nights, a Center School parent who taught at a local high school tried the same assignment with her literature class. Despite a year with them in which they studied hard and well together, she reported that it failed. An essential ingredient was missing, she realized. That ingredient was trust.

They knew how to write dialogue and paint sets. But sharing things of import to them and trusting in a respectful response— that was another level entirely. In the end, the plays were superficial and the students' commitment to them half-hearted.

Are the Center School plays the product of one year of literature study? Only in part. True, they emerge with the help of an inspiring teacher, at a transitional moment when students are keenly aware of their impending graduation and are poised to look back as they step ahead. But it is also true that they are the product of a group of students who have practiced the Morning Meeting skills of communication and community every day of their school lives for as much as nine years.

They have used their voices to greet, sing, laugh, console, and celebrate within their Meeting circles for all those mornings of all those years. And on Play Night, those voices join an ensemble and speak, not just to each other across the circle, but to the larger audience which they face from the stage. They are oh-so-ready. And Morning Meeting helped get them there.

Morning Meeting merges social, emotional, and intellectual learning.

Morning Meeting provides an arena where distinctions that define social, emotional and academic skills fade, and learning becomes an integrated experience. Parker Palmer describes his vision of an educational community as one that depends on a dynamic dialogue about things that matter. He states, "Truth is an eternal conversation about things that matter, conducted with passion and discipline. . . . But it is not our knowledge of conclusions that keeps us in the truth. It is our commitment to the conversation itself, our willingness to put forward our observations and interpretations for testing by the community and to return the favor to others. To be in the truth, we must know how to observe and reflect and speak and listen, with passion and with discipline, in the circle gathered around a given subject." (Palmer 1998, 104)

In Morning Meeting the circle "gathers around" many subjects, some introduced by the teacher, some by the children. In the dialogue of the circle, we stretch each others' understandings, using the skills which Palmer names: observing, reflecting, speaking, listening.

A consulting teacher tells of a Morning Meeting she led in a classroom she visited in a distant city. The newspaper headline that morning told of a citywide water contamination crisis. At Morning Meeting, she shared that she had seen that headline and asked these third-graders what they knew about the water problem in their city.

Her question triggered an outpouring of knowledge. They knew, in fact, a great deal. She listened and noted the facts on a chart. As the listing of what they knew reached an end, the talk turned to what they didn't know but wondered about. Those questions, too, were noted on the chart, along with some hypotheses. Another teacher from the school observed the Meeting and was incredulous. "Those kids must have been rehearsed; they couldn't know that much!"

This conversation, within the structured safety of Morning Meeting, allowed learners to put forward what conclusions they knew, to pose questions and venture possible interpretations. They were able to "observe and reflect and speak and listen" communally about a subject that mattered very much to them.

In the wonderful book *On Their Way,* listening and talking are deemed "the power tools." (Fraser and Skolnick 1994, 145) Recognizing this, many school systems now endorse cooperative learning activities and approaches in classrooms, and there is much talk about the skills of collaboration needed to move into the next decades. Morning Meeting sharpens the tools of listening and talking which are essential for partner chats, small group discussions, peer critiquing, and other cooperative learning strategies.

See *Appendix A: What Children Are Learning in Each Component of Morning Meeting* for a full listing of the myriad social, emotional, and intellectual skills children are learning as they gather together in Morning Meeting.

GETTING STARTED

Establish a set schedule for Morning Meeting.

Morning Meeting must happen every day. The best time is first thing in the morning after most children have arrived and settled in. Schedule 15–30 minutes for Morning Meeting, depending upon the age of the children in your class. You may wish to reconsider your schedule as the year progresses. The class that squirmed their way raggedly through ten minutes of meeting time in September may be quite ready for double that time by November.

It is important, even with older students, to keep Morning Meetings from going on too long. It is also important to plan for a

Morning Meeting sharpens children's
speaking and listening skills.

change of pace immediately following Morning Meeting. When it is followed by an academic period requiring continued sitting in a circle, it can be deadly for even the most focused and attentive students. Even a few minutes of an activity which requires some moving around provides the needed variation.

Many teachers of young children have found that a separate "Sharing" meeting at a predictable time later in the day is more productive. The attention and focus that students can give each other during Sharing is more important than the time of day that it happens.

Introduce Morning Meeting to your students.

Explain to students that you will begin each day with a meeting—Morning Meeting. Share with them your hopes and goals for this part of the day. Your list might sound something like this:

- I hope that we will all get to know one another—not just our best friends.

- I want us to be able to practice taking care of each other so that we can all feel good about being in this class.

- I want us to be able to share different experiences and ideas.

- I want us to have fun together.

If your students are already familiar with Morning Meeting from previous years, ask them to share their hopes and goals for this part of the day.

Communicate with parents about Morning Meeting.

Parents are very supportive of Morning Meeting when they understand its format and goals. If their first impression is formed from a child's report of a "new game we played at Morning Meeting," they may draw the mistaken conclusion that this is time taken away from learning. A letter to parents giving them a glimpse of this part of their child's day and describing the learning integral to it, can give them a framework in which to place the accounts they hear from their children. Good communication will help parents see Morning Meeting for the vital learning time that it is.

A sample, "boilerplate" letter is included in *Appendix B*. Feel free to use it as a template, adapting it to your school and your class. You might also consider talking about Morning Meeting at a Parent Night, or PTA meeting, maybe even structuring a piece of the parents' meeting in Morning Meeting format. Encourage parents to visit the classroom and join in a Morning Meeting.

Phase in the implementation of Morning Meeting.

Acquaint your class with one component of Morning Meeting at a time, introducing and modeling each. (See the *Getting Started* section for each component in the following chapters.) When you sense that students are comfortable and ready for more, then add a component. Though this isn't their eventual order, the most successful order of introduction is: Greeting, Group Activity, News and Announcements, and Sharing.

A plan for the first day might involve teaching children how to get to and into a circle, and then singing a song. On the second day, a greeting might be taught after the circle has formed. A few days later, the Morning Message chart might be introduced with a message as simple as "Welcome." Full Morning Meeting might not happen for several weeks.

Factors like the age and school experience of your students will influence your decision about timing. Your knowledge of your class will determine how quickly you add components. A carefully paced and deliberate introduction of new components, with time to practice and reflect, will pay off in the end.

Choose and teach signals you will use consistently.

It is essential to have simple, effective signals to get students' attention. Raising your voice is often neither simple nor effective, and if students are still involved in conversation or activity, chances are that many will not absorb the announcement.

Instead, teachers have found various non-verbal signals that say to students: "Stop what you are doing and give me (or a student who may be about to make an announcement) your attention." Some teachers ring a chime, bell, or triangle; others turn the classroom lights off, then on. When you have the attention of all students, make a brief statement. "Five minutes till Morning Meeting. Put away what you are working on and come to the Meeting area."

A "hands up" signal is useful to bring quiet and attention once the Meeting circle is formed. These signals are not exclusively for teacher use, but are available for responsible use by students as well. The same respect and response is expected whether a signal originates with a student or teacher, as in the following example.

It is Jonas' turn to share. He brought his gerbil, Harry, who has been waiting in his cage on a table in the corner. When Jonas leaves the circle to get Harry, many conversations commence. Jonas comes back, ready to share, but his classmates continue to chatter. He raises his hand. Across the circle, Amanda notices and raises hers. She gently elbows Leisha, next to her, who is whispering to Damien. Up goes Leisha's hand and she stops in mid-sentence

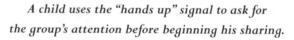

A child uses the "hands up" signal to ask for the group's attention before beginning his sharing.

and looks at Jonas. Around the circle hands go up and silence spreads. It is simple and efficient, with not a word of scolding or blame issued. His audience is ready and Jonas begins. "This is Harry. He's really a she. . ."

The logistics of Morning Meeting are important. Consider and teach them carefully.

Over and over in our teaching lives, we are reminded not to make assumptions about what children know. Details about forming the circle for Morning Meeting and about coming to the circle with hands empty demand careful instruction at the outset and vigilant monitoring even when routines are established.

Understanding the "why" behind the details helps. Discuss why the circle is important to Morning Meeting. Talk about why it's important not to be clicking pens and rustling papers during Morning Meeting.

These discussions vary with the ages and readiness of students. I have heard six-year-olds offer simple and profound explanations: "A circle makes it possible for every person to see every other person. It has no front or back." I have heard twelve-year-olds engage in thoughtful and sophisticated discussions about different classroom arrangements—desks in rows, lecture halls, round seminar tables—and what sort of activity each promotes.

Many classes sit on the floor for Morning Meeting. Other classes seem to handle themselves better, or feel recognized as older, when seated in chairs. There is no single correct way. What's important is that the circle creates an open and inviting space which allows for a group activity and encourages a comfortable but attentive attitude.

If students need to move furniture to clear a space large enough for the whole class to make a circle, or if they need to move their chairs over to the circle area, talk about how it can be done smoothly.

"We will need to move our chairs in a way that takes care of our room and the people in it. What are some things we will need to think about so

that we can do it safely and efficiently?"poses the teacher to her third grade
class.

"Not scuffing the floors."

"Be careful not to hit anybody with your chair by accident."

"Put chairs down softly so we don't bother the kindergartners on the
first floor."

A bit of modeling helps. "Show me, Shannon, how you can get your
chair into the circle in a way that does all those things we just talked
about. What do you think, class?" Practice it. Reflect about how it went.
"Let's time ourselves. Was it safe? Was it efficient? On a scale of 1–5, rate
how we managed it."(For more about how to use modeling as a teaching strategy, see *Appendix C.*)

Meeting rules vary depending on the age and needs of a group. The
rules on the left were generated by a group of first graders, and the
rules on the right were created by a group of fifth and sixth graders.

Generate Morning Meeting rules with the students.

After students are comfortable with a couple of the components of Morning Meeting, refer to the goals named and pose a question which will establish a basic set of meeting procedures. "How can we take care of ourselves and each other so that our hopes for Morning Meeting can happen? What will we need to do?"

Implicit in the stance of this question is a view of rules as a social necessity generated by the community involved, not an arbitrary and disconnected list of do's and don'ts. Answers will likely include some variation of the following:

- Listen
- Look at the person who's talking
- Keep your body in control
- Raise your hand if you want to talk
- Keep your hands down when someone is speaking
- Don't laugh at anyone

For many of the rules, a definition of terms is in order. Children are much more able to follow rules when they are defined in concrete terms.

"Listen!" volunteers a kindergartner.

"And how will someone who's speaking know that you're listening?" asks his teacher. A discussion of some of the finer points of listening etiquette follows: your eyes are on the person; you try not to wiggle; if you have to go to the bathroom, you try to wait until the person is done talking. Indeed, those are hallmarks of quality listening for five- and six-year-olds.

"Be respectful," offers a ten-year-old earnestly. "For sure," endorses her teacher. "And how do people show respect in a meeting?"

When a simple list and a common understanding of the rules have been reached, a poster with these rules displayed near the Meeting area can be a helpful reminder.

Give students responsibility in Morning Meeting.

Virtually every moment in Morning Meeting is laden with opportunities for students to assume responsibility in the community we call our classroom. They are responsible for making someone feel welcome, asking a thoughtful question, making a kind comment, solving a "puzzler" question on the chart. In some classrooms, once Morning Meeting is familiar and established, students also take turns leading the whole Meeting or selected parts of it.

We must give our students real responsibility in Morning Meeting; we must believe that they can be trusted and will be successful in meeting the expectations we hold. This can be difficult, particularly for those of us who gained much of our experience in more teacher-centered settings. We may be accustomed to being the dispensers of information and the handers-out of papers. It can be a tricky business to step back from the center, while remaining in control.

Pay attention to your role as teacher.

Make no mistake: successful Morning Meetings require a teacher who is in control in the classroom. As teachers we are interpreters, synthesizers, balance-keepers, time-keepers, and safety-net holders. Even when students are leading a section of Meeting, we are watchful and often intervene with a re-framing question, a quick suggestion, or redirection.

What is required of us in this role may be simple and straightforward. "Choose one more person for a question or comment, Danita," we say when many hands are raised and time is running short; "Join the circle, Todd," to a boy who always wants to hang back.

Other times, discerning and guiding the dynamics in Morning Meeting can be more complex. Jeremy continually shares complicated details of "scary science" stories about mutant viruses, colliding asteroids, and toxic pesticides which invisibly saturate

Meetings are rich with opportunities for students to assume
responsibility. In some classes, children may take turns
leading some or all of the Meeting.

strawberries. He is a highly knowledgeable child and his graphic details are accurate and documented.

His teacher wonders about the effect of this stream of threatening news, so authoritatively presented, upon his eleven-year-old peers. Are they terrified, challenged, or humiliated by their relative lack of factual knowledge? Is this a positive way for Jeremy to define a niche in the class? Careful observation and perhaps a one-on-one chat with Jeremy outside of Meeting will inform his teacher as she contemplates whether her intervention is needed to protect either Jeremy or the class.

Bob Strachota, author and teacher at the Greenfield Center School, tells a story of a child he coached in soccer who commented, "I like how you taught us soccer. You were always in the middle, but never in the way." The teacher's role in Morning Meeting is a bit like that. We are not the center, but we are central.

**Pay attention to the management aspects of Morning
Meeting and hold children to the expectations you have
named together.**

Addressing what can seem like small details—whom students
greet, where they sit, which students are rarely the recipients of
thoughtful comments—sends two messages: you value the skills
and attitudes that specific actions reflect and you believe in the
capacity of your students to accomplish them.

For Morning Meeting to flourish, we must let children know
that we are as serious about their behavior and skills during this
time as we are during reading group or math group. Let them
know by your comments that you notice how they are doing with
the named expectations, and that you will hold them to those
expectations, helping them by reminders and directions when they
need them. Frame your comments in the positive, focusing upon
what students are doing right, or upon helping them identify what
would be a better way, rather than naming what it is they are not
doing.

You may think of these sorts of comments as the "three R's"—
reinforcing, reminding, or redirecting comments. Here are some
examples:

Reinforcing

- I notice the way everyone remembered to smile at the person they greeted today.

- I notice lots of people sitting next to different classmates each day.

- Most people are remembering to read the message chart when they enter our room in the morning.

- I notice how quickly and quietly we moved our chairs into a circle this morning.

Reminding

- Before we move to the Meeting rug, remind me what you will think about as you choose where to sit.
- Who remembers what to do if you forget the name of someone you want to greet?
- Laurie, remind me, what do we need to remember as we move our chairs into the circle?

Redirecting

- I hear a lot of chair legs dragging across the floor. Show me, Jonah, how we can hold our chairs when we move them so that they don't scuff the floor.
- Today you must sit next to someone of the opposite gender, Cheryl.
- I see that a lot of people are looking at things that others brought for Sharing. Show me where we could put these things so that we can give our attention to the person speaking.

Morning Meeting Responsibilities

In implementing and assessing Morning Meeting, keep the following general responsibilities in mind.

Teachers' responsibilities

- **To make sure the space is adequate and appropriate for the component. Can a circle form? Can all be seen? Can a particular game be safely played?**
- **To act as timekeeper, keeping things moving**
- **To facilitate the Meeting, making sure that all children are greeted, that a variety of children are responding to sharing, that the tone is respectful, etc.**

- To observe students' skills—both social and academic

- To notice behaviors and to reinforce, remind, and redirect using positive language

- To make sure that there is equal opportunity to participate, that gender or personality traits aren't dictating participation patterns

- To make sure everyone in the classroom (parapro-fessionals, visitors, parents, etc.) is included in the Meeting

Students' responsibilities

- To get to Meeting promptly and to form the circle safely and efficiently

- To participate fully—contributing actively, listening well, and responding appropriately

- To interact with a variety of classmates in the good spirit of Morning Meeting

- To move smoothly from Meeting to the next activity

FINE TUNINGS

Most of my students really are great at Morning Meeting, but a couple of my students just can't sit still and behave themselves. How can I help them be part of Meeting and not disrupt it?

Children vary a great deal in their ability to follow Meeting rules. The teacher's knowledge of the individual involved is the starting point for any action. Is the child younger than most peers and simply not yet ready for the expectations that are appropriate for the rest of the group? Are there special needs making participation particularly challenging?

For the child, particularly in primary rooms, who is simply young, making a special arrangement about the length of time he attends Morning Meeting makes sense. Make a signal that will let him know when he is to leave the circle and discuss his options in the room for the remaining Meeting time. Gradually, as he is successful, extend the time he spends in Meeting.

Sometimes a bit of situational assistance is all that is needed. "Miranda, I notice that you have a hard time listening to other people when you sit next to Molly. You need to pick a different place to sit at Morning Meeting."

Or to the fidgeter whose fancy, gizmo-watch treats everyone to a rendition of three electronic verses of "The Yellow Rose of Texas" at least twice in every Meeting, "Your watch needs to be in your cubby during Morning Meeting, Gerard."

A few children with lots of overflowing energy are better able to concentrate by being allowed to bring something that quietly occupies their hands to Meeting. Is this fair, some may ask, when the rule is to come to Meeting empty-handed? This is a complex question about justice that repeats itself with variations all through our lives.

Fair treatment is responsive to individual needs and doesn't always mean treating people with a cookie-cutter sameness. When students trust that their needs, too, will be met in the same spirit of fairness, they are generally able to understand and accept these modifications.

Occasionally a child's special needs require more elaborate intervention. I saw a skillful example of this a few years ago in a fourth/fifth grade inclusion classroom. Andrew was a fifth-grader whose special needs manifested in blurting out inappropriate and rude remarks often unconnected to anything preceding them. Early in the first weeks of the school year, it was clear that he was not ready to be part of group sharing, that he needed some very specialized and intensive instruction in order to participate in this part of Meeting.

So, every day, when it was time for Sharing, Andrew and one of his teachers, Ms. Scamardella (Ms. S.), left the circle and moved to a table in the opposite corner of the room where Andrew had "private sharing" with Ms. S. while co-teacher Ms. Daggett continued the Meeting. In his "private sharing," Andrew practiced sharing a piece of news appropriately, with no swearing or name-calling. Ms. S. modeled careful patterns of suitable responses. Then she shared a piece of news and helped him learn to choose a polite response and practice it.

After a few months Andrew was able to rejoin the group for Sharing, listening quietly most days, and on a really good day, offering a comment or a question "on the spot." Andrew's own sharing to the group was scheduled for Friday each week, sharing which he planned and rehearsed a few minutes each day, Monday through Thursday, with Ms. S.

This example is more extreme than most, but it illustrates a couple of important principles. Just as different groups are ready for the phasing in of Morning Meeting components at different rates, individual children may be ready at different rates also. While children should participate in Morning Meeting as much as they can with as little modification as possible, if their participation is "stuck" in the negative, if they are spending more time in the time-out chair than in the Meeting circle, then clearly the teacher must pay special attention and address the situation.

I have several children who frequently come in late, and a couple who have to leave in the middle of Meeting for special programs. Should they be part of Meeting?

Yes, definitely. Morning Meeting is for everyone. Latecomers should be greeted pleasantly and welcomed without unduly disrupting whatever is happening in Meeting. In order to minimize the disruption while still making the latecomer feel welcome, some teachers assign a child the daily job of welcoming latecomers into the circle.

Meeting time itself is not the time to address the tardiness, frustrating as it may be. If it is an occasional lateness, simply help the child fit into the flow of the day. If it is a chronic problem with a particular child, then some investigation is in order. Do they walk to school? Dawdle once they're in the building? Do parents drop them off on the way to work?

Sometimes a chat with the student alone is enough; other times parents' help is needed. And sometimes, no matter how many phone calls and discussions of the importance of beginning the day with the class and how promptness implicitly communicates respect and responsibility, there is little progress.

In the case of students who have to leave early for "specials," make sure that Greeting can happen with them in the circle, and teach them how to leave the circle quietly and unobtrusively when it is time. If the same students must leave every day, you might think about scheduling a separate "Sharing" meeting near the end of the day when everyone can attend. And for younger children who are not yet able to read the chart independently, make sure they are aware of news and announcements for the day.

Children are really comfortable with our Morning Meeting, maybe too comfortable. Even I sometimes feel like it's boring. Help!

This is one of the areas where the teacher acts as a "balancer." There is a sensitive balance between the lovely sense of security that routine can provide and the monotony that can creep in when that routine is unlivened and unleavened. As classes grow comfortable with each other and with the basic format of Morning Meeting, we must introduce variation.

Ruth Charney speaks about the perils of overscriptedness: "Sometimes I build Morning Meeting primarily around a game, after a quick greeting. Or I might stress discussion about Current Events my students are clearly interested in. Our students are all differently abled and they shine in different parts of Meeting. I find that once a group is comfortable with the order and structure of Morning Meeting, then varying the pace, tempo, and proportion of structures is essential lest comfort turn to complacency, or worse yet, contempt."

Children in my classroom usually choose to sit next to their friends. Any ideas for making this work better?

Calling this to students' attention, within the context of the larger purposes of Morning Meeting, is often enough intervention. "I notice," says the teacher, "that for the last several mornings, many of us have been choosing to sit next to our good friends. Remember that one of the purposes of Morning Meeting is to help us get to know and feel comfortable with everyone—including those who are not already our friends. Think about that when you choose where you will sit this morning at Meeting." Tying what may seem a superficial detail to the grander vision we hold, to the underlying significance, helps students see why it merits attention.

Sometimes formalizing these expectations into seating cues is necessary. "Boys next to girls" and "new friends' day" can be useful shorthand for reminding students of our expectations and shaping the options a bit, when needed.

There are also ways to arrange seating which engineer different mixes and shake up entrenched patterns. In some primary classes, students make and decorate "sit-upons" with their names, which teachers rotate often so that children sit next to many class members. In older classes, you might want to start with a round of "The Cold Wind Blows" *(Appendix E),* a very quick game which will shake up the seating arrangement.

At certain developmental stages, issues of gender and friendship are at the fore. Recently, I visited in a fifth/sixth grade classroom where the students assembled themselves into a circle on their Meeting rug that was a clear sociogram. Girls sat next to girls and boys next to boys. A couple of clear "best friends" clusters could be identified by the shoulder-to-shoulder huddled posture they assumed. The circle was ragged, with two children sitting considerably back from the rest.

The teacher took his place in the circle and looked around quietly. "Meeting seating, please," he announced, and as if they were accomplished square dancers responding to a call, the students arose and wound their way around and across the circle, pausing to survey the scene before sitting again, cross-legged, on the floor. The circle was now a circle, students sitting boy-girl-boy-girl evenly distributed around its perimeter. "Good Morning!" smiled their teacher and the Meeting began.

Scripted? Certainly. But sometimes it's our job to provide a script when the one the students have created is destructive to the group. After an initial and mandatory groan, these students didn't object. They were testing a limit and were relieved to find that, yes, it was still there. There are some ages at which this structure would not be necessary and some ages at which it would not be tolerated and would cause a reaction more problematic than helpful. For this particular group, at that point in their development, it was just right.

In my classroom, there is a child nobody wants to sit next to. How should I address this?

Frequently students deliberately ostracize a certain child, the social outcast of the group, by not sitting next to her. Action is required on two fronts—one immediate, the other longer term.

First, do whatever you must to stop the exclusion-by-seating. Remove the element of choice by assigning seating patterns that rotate (see previous question). Or assign partners who will sit together at Morning Meeting and work together during any partner activities within the Meeting.

Identifying why the particular child is not accepted and working with her and others in the group to remedy that is clearly a long-term project. Sometimes, assigning or reading a book chosen for its relevant plot can help prompt a "safe" discussion of a social issue such as exclusion.

Helping a child overcome this kind of reputation, especially when there is a long and entrenched history, is tough. Making sure that all classroom members include her respectfully in the seating and other routines of Morning Meeting is an important start.

What is the difference between Class Meetings and Morning Meetings?

Class Meetings are held for the purpose of solving a problem, or perhaps planning for a project or event or de-briefing afterwards. They are generally not held every day, but perhaps weekly, or as needed.

Morning Meetings are held for the purposes named earlier and are held every day. They are not used as a time to solve problems or take care of general classroom business. Teachers who use both kinds of meetings often comment that many of the habits of participation and social skills that are developed through Morning Meeting help their students in democratic, cooperative processes like Class Meetings.

Is it important that I do the components in the order you suggest?

Yes. The order of the four components—Greeting, Sharing, Group Activity, and News and Announcements—matters (although they are introduced in a different order, as covered earlier). Greeting serves as a logical warm-up and tone-setter for Sharing, which requires that students feel a sense of comfort and trust in the group. The group must be feeling settled and calm in order for Sharing to work well. We've often seen teachers do Sharing after the Group Activity or News and Announcements and then wonder why the students weren't able to listen well or ask focused and thoughtful questions.

The Group Activity follows Sharing because at this point in the Meeting the children are ready for the liveliness which whole-group involvement brings. News and Announcements helps to bring the group back to a more calm stance after the liveliness of Activity and serves as a transition to the rest of the school day.

Greeting

A FRIENDLY AND

RESPECTFUL SALUTE

"Good Morning, Morgan."
Hector speaks seriously and earnestly, for that is who Hector is. He looks directly at Morgan, who sits on his left, and offers his right hand.

"Good Morning, Hector!" returns Morgan. He grins widely and grasps Hector's hand with exuberance. Morgan's "Good mornings" are always punctuated with invisible exclamation points, for that is who Morgan is.

Shannon, on Morgan's left, shifts a bit and sits up taller, ready to receive the enthusiasm of a greeting, Morgan-style. And here it comes. "Good Morning, Shannon!" "Good Morning, Morgan!" Her teacher smiles, pleased with Shannon's strong voice and firm hand-shake. Shannon had entered the third grade classroom in September with a tentative air. Everything about her seemed designed to help her escape the notice of her peers—the accept-able, regulation clothes in quiet colors, her fade-into-the-chair posture, her barely audible voice at Meetings. Now, four months and more than seventy Morning Meetings later, here she is, wear-ing a smile almost as broad as Morgan's above her bright purple-and-red-striped turtleneck, her hand extended and waiting for his.

Greeting can be simple and straightforward. Here, kindergartners pass a handshake greeting around the circle.

And so it goes around the circle. Greeting takes slightly less than three minutes. Every member of the circle—children, teacher, assistant teacher, and Matthew's mother, who is visiting this morning—has been greeted by name, with a handshake and eye contact.

Purposes and Reflections

Morning Meetings begin with Greeting. Even on days when there isn't time for a full Morning Meeting, teachers convene the circle and make sure Greeting takes place. It is that important because of the tone it sets and the way that tone carries into the rest of the day.

Some mornings, Greeting is basic and straightforward. Variations might be simple, such as students tossing a ball to the student whom they are greeting, or substituting a "high five" for the handshake. Other mornings, the greeting process is more elaborate or complex, perhaps fanciful. It might be a call-and-response greeting, or a greeting that requires students to offer an adjective describing themselves and beginning with the same letter as their name. Some Greetings work with all ages; others have features that make them appropriate only for younger grades or have complex steps better suited to older students.

Long or short, dignified or playful, Greetings share four common purposes which are explored in the sections which follow.

Purposes of Greeting

- **Sets a positive tone**
- **Provides a sense of recognition and belonging**
- **Helps children learn names**
- **Gives practice in offering hospitality**

Greeting sets a positive tone for the classroom and the day.

To greet, according to Webster, is to "salute or welcome in a friendly and respectful way." Welcoming, friendly, respectful—those are attributes which characterize the climate in exemplary classrooms. Beginning Morning Meeting with Greeting helps create such a climate.

The fact that there is a designated Greeting each day is important. Though there is great room for individual personality to infuse the greeting—Hector's "Good morning" is different from Morgan's which is different from Shannon's—there is also an equity and a safety in having a structure for the greeting. It is unlike the spontaneous, informal way we offer greetings based on our immediate feelings: our close friends get warm smiles; acquaintances get more neutral hellos; those with whom we struggle to get along may get only a perfunctory nod. The goal in Morning Meeting Greeting is for *all* to greet and be greeted equally. Within a classroom community, starting a day by hearing your name spoken with respect and warmth is not a privilege which lands upon just the popular few—those social successes who seem born knowing

which T-shirts with what logos are in this year, knowing how to say
"Hey. . ." with just the right inflection and number of syllables
instead of "Hi." It is, instead, a right to which all are entitled. When
we make time for Greeting every morning, no matter how full the
schedule, we make a statement as teachers that we expect respect
and equity and that we will do our best to make sure it happens.

**Being greeted provides a sense of recognition and
belonging which meets a universal human need.**

In *The Fifth Discipline Fieldbook* (Senge 1994, 3), Peter Senge tells of
the most common greeting among the tribes of Natal in South
Africa. The greeting, *Sawu Bona,* translates literally as "I see you."
The standard reply is *Sikhona,* literally "I am here." The order of

*Greeting can also be more elaborate or complex, perhaps even
fanciful. Here, a group of fourth graders tries out a puppet greeting.*

these phrases is important and not variable. One cannot be there until one is seen. The truth of this extends beyond linguistic convention.

My student Sue (whom you met in the Introduction) went ungreeted and unseen for seven-eighths of her day. Unseen, she felt she was not there. Because she was old enough to do something about it, she chose to physically remove herself. Sadly, our classrooms have too many other children who, though physically present, walk through their days feeling unacknowledged and unseen, feeling they aren't really there.

I think of the old expression "neither here nor there." It means "unimportant and irrelevant," the opposite of how we want our students to feel. We want them to feel important and relevant. We want them to be "here." And so they must feel seen. The act of intentional greeting helps us to see and be seen.

Greeting helps children learn and use each others' names.

To know someone's name and to feel comfortable using it provides powerful options. It lets us call upon each other. It is a way we get each others' attention, enabling us to ask a question, to recognize one another in a discussion, to request help, to offer congratulations or whisper an apology.

We can't assume that because students are grouped together they will learn each others' names. Last year a colleague returned from meeting with a group of middle school teachers who had asked him to come and speak with them about Responsive Classroom strategies at the middle school level. With fewer than two hundred students comprising the seventh and eighth grades, this regional school was not large, though students from several adjacent towns met for the first time in seventh grade. The faculty wanted to build a sense of community among their students and teachers, and had been using a heterogeneous team-based approach to organize their school for several years.

One of the teachers mentioned in conversation that just the day before he had asked a student in his math class to hand back a set of papers and she couldn't do it. Why? She didn't know all of her classmates' names, couldn't match the names at the top of the papers with the faces of her peers. It was mid-January and this was a team of students who had been together in many classes using cooperative learning strategies since September.

A student who doesn't know her classmates well enough to hand them their work is unlikely to feel familiar enough with them to offer her dissenting opinion about a character in a short story or admit that she doesn't quite get this business of "3 is to 21 as x is to 28" or share a poem she wrote about her grandmother. And what a loss that is for her and for her classmates.

Much of our learning happens through social interaction. Knowing names is a fundamental building block for those interactions. It is why name tags at workshops are such a help and one of the reasons why substitute teachers, faced with twenty-five students they may have never seen before and cannot address by name, often feel so powerless. Naming is often the beginning of knowing.

Hearing our name is also a reminder of our identity, our individualness within the group. As members of a community, we regularly identify with larger groups. For example, we are all "Center Schoolers" at our weekly All-School Meeting when we cheer for our soccer team and we are members of a smaller group, such as the Prime Reds, at the end of the meeting when classes are dismissed one-by-one. Although it's important that we feel a part of this larger community, it's also essential that we retain a sense of individuality as well. Hearing our name lets us know that someone values speaking to us as an individual and wants our attention. Our name allows us to claim authorship when we are proud of what we have created, a stamp that lets the world know we exist and that what we have done is important.

Only one word or phrase names and identifies each of us as an individual. When my son went to preschool, he was one of three

Bens in a class of twelve. When someone called "Hey, Ben!" from the snack table, three boys would respond. None of them wished to be a Benjie or a Benjamin, so they quickly became Ben K, Ben G, and Ben P. Two years later, about to enter kindergarten, Ben wondered aloud, "Think I'll be the only Ben in my new class?" He arrived home after the first day to tell me that things had improved a little. There were only two Bens in this class. He remained Ben K and it became so ingrained in his identity that my Mother's Day cards were signed "Ben K" for years.

Greeting gives children a chance to practice the art of offering hospitality.

"Hospitality is always an act that benefits the host even more than the guest. The concept of hospitality arose in ancient times when this reciprocity was easier to see: in nomadic cultures, the food and shelter one gave to a stranger yesterday is the food and shelter one hopes to receive from a stranger tomorrow. By offering hospitality, one participates in the endless reweaving of a social fabric on which all can depend." (Palmer 1998, 50)

Welcoming each other to our classroom every day is an act of hospitality. The offering of that welcome, one to another, affirms that we are caretakers of each other in that community. Being a host also implies, builds, and strengthens a person's ownership and investment in that place.

We practice daily the skills of welcoming each other—the clear voice, the friendly smile, the careful remembering that Nicholas likes to be called Nick, the firm handshake. When guests visit and are part of our circle, we extend a welcome to them as well, although it can feel a bit awkward at first. "Should we call her Carol or Mrs. DiAngelo?" whispers Andy to his teacher when he notices that his friend Matt's mother is coming to Morning Meeting. "Could you check with her and see which would feel more comfortable to her?" replies his teacher.

Several important messages are conveyed in this suggestion.

First, there is no one right answer to that question in our culture these days. Some parents prefer that children use their first names; others deem it disrespectful. Second, the role of a host is to make the guest feel respected and comfortable. And third, asking a polite and direct question is a fine way to get an answer you need. It is practice in assertiveness seasoned with courtesy, not an easy blend to get right at any age.

Kindergarten teacher Eileen Mariani of Erving Elementary School in Millers Falls, Massachusetts, is proud of a January morning in her room.

The habit of greeting within the Morning Meeting circle had been well established. On that particular morning it was Isaac's turn to be Morning Meeting leader. Isaac was a shy boy who approached his role as leader with some trepidation. Eileen watched carefully, ready to help if Isaac seemed worried at any point. But, no need, he was doing splendidly.

He had chosen "Good Morning, Friends" (Appendix D) for the Greeting and it had been clapped and stamped with a nicely modulated glee around the circle, just returning to Isaac, when Isaac glanced up and stood abruptly, heading for the door. Eileen, whose view of the door was blocked by a bookshelf, also

These fifth graders practice the skills of "respectful" greeting: making eye contact, shaking hands gently, saying the person's name clearly.

rose to survey what was going on. There stood Isaac, framed by the doorway, hand extended to a distinguished-looking visitor who was entering the room with the principal. "Good morning, Mr....Uh...I'm sorry, what is your name please?" Isaac proceeded to shake the visitor's hand before walking gravely back to his place on the rug to continue the Meeting.

The months of modeling and practicing, the discussions of "What can you do if you don't remember someone's name?" had taken hold and enabled Isaac to extend graceful hospitality, not just beyond Morning Meeting with classmates, but even to a stranger at the door. Isaac's extended hand was a true act of welcome and hospitality.

Highlights of Greeting

- Ensures that every child names and notices others at the outset of the day

- Allows the teacher to observe and "take the pulse" of the group that day

- Provides practice in elements of greeting such as making eye contact and shaking hands

- Requires students to extend the range of classmates they spontaneously notice and greet

- Helps students to reach across gender, clique, and friendship lines that form at particular ages

- Can employ strategies which challenge the intellect (patterns, acquisition of foreign language phrases, set making, calculating fractions)

- Encourages clear and audible speech

You may want to browse through or study *Appendix D,* which lists and describes a wide range of Greetings, to get a sense of their variety and content before continuing on to the next section.

GETTING STARTED

Begin by introducing Greeting.

Choosing your language carefully when introducing Greeting establishes expectations from the outset. "We are going to learn to do lots of different friendly and respectful greetings," states the teacher, before going on to model what she means by those two adjectives.

The teacher turns to Sara and greets her, then asks the class, "What did you notice?"

"You said her name."

"You looked at her."

"You took her hand."

"Sara, what did you notice about the way I held your hand?"

Specific behaviors are noted and named, becoming part of a classroom lexicon. You might write on the chart as you summarize, "So, a friendly greeting means saying a person's name, looking at them, and shaking their hand in a gentle way."

As always, language and focus will vary with the age of the children in the group. With older children, focusing on the "respectful" aspect is often more useful. Even the most entrenched adolescents who argue that their choice of friends is their own business will acknowledge that all of us are entitled to respectful treatment.

Always begin by modeling and practicing the positive ways of greeting. Then, depending on the make-up of your class, you may want to insert some of the more subtle gestures that children frequently try out. You might mumble a person's name, pump a hand exaggeratedly, or look at the clock while greeting a child. "How did I or didn't I show respect?" The details matter. We know that; they know that. Modeling and discussion helps them know that we know.

Keep Greeting simple at first.

When first introducing Greeting to a group, or at the year's start when a new group is getting to know each other, simple, direct Greetings work best. The teacher models "greeting," calling attention to important qualities of the greeting—names spoken clearly, greeter and greeted looking directly at each other, friendly handshakes and voices. When students are able to fluently go around the circle saying "Good morning" to each other, then it's time to introduce various other Greetings *(Appendix D)*.

This example illustrates how Sandra Norried of Washington, D.C., a masterful and experienced third grade teacher, offers her class just the right amount of choice.

For the first weeks of school, Ms. N. has chosen the Greeting and now, in October, is beginning to hand that choice over to students. She knows from her years of teaching, however, that too many choices can be as limiting as too few, especially when the year is young. So for this week, the leader will not choose the Greeting itself, but one element of it—a rhythm instrument. Each instrument has been introduced, one per day, and now there are six to choose from.

"Today Sienna will lead our Greeting. Sienna, what will you use?"

Ms. N. hands Sienna a blue crate containing an assortment of rhythm instruments. Sienna studies the possibilities intently for a moment before reaching in to make her choice. Gently, with the slightest of jingles, she produces a tambourine and holds it aloft for her classmates to see. A collective grin spreads around the circle. The tambourine is clearly a favorite of these third-graders.

The Greeting moves clockwise around the circle. After each "Good morning," the greeter shakes the tambourine before passing it to the greeted. Some shake it tentatively and softly; others brandish it above their heads, with extended and elaborated rhythms involving their whole bodies.

This kind of boundary-setting helps to define space for learning, something teachers do constantly in their planning—deciding how far apart to place the cones on the play yard for tag games, which books to set out on the Choice Reading Shelf, how many choices to make available for greetings. Ideally we set boundaries far enough apart that they allow ample room for exploration and experimentation, but not so wide that they allow students to get lost.

Help students learn each others' names.

Name tags, either prepared ahead by the teacher, or made by students, are a great help in the early days of a new group. There are also many games and activities which focus upon learning names *(Appendices D and E)* and are very helpful in the early days. With young children, starting the year with chorus greetings in which everyone says or sings the names together can help the children feel comfortable and help them learn each others' names. When the children are ready to say names individually, making pairs ahead of Greeting so that each is prepared to say a partner's name can help boost children's confidence.

Anticipate and help students handle awkward moments.

Many Greetings require students to choose the person they will greet, rather than simply proceeding around the circle in order. This requires participants to pay attention in order to remember who has and hasn't been named. Teachers can help by modeling what to do in those inevitable moments when, despite their best efforts, students can't remember a name or who has already been greeted. "What can you say if you forget someone's name?" "What can you say if you forget who has been greeted?" Some teachers work out a signal—such as thumbs up until you're greeted—with their class. Such signals help the last few greeters who may be struggling to remember who remains to be greeted.

Greeting Responsibilities

In implementing and assessing Greeting, keep the following general responsibilities in mind.

Teachers' responsibilities

- Teach a variety of age-appropriate Greetings
- Model aspects of warm and respectful greeting
- Make sure children use friendly and appropriate words and body language

- **Give students opportunities to choose and lead Greetings**

Students' responsibilities

- **Choose different classmates each day to greet**
- **Wait for their turn to greet**
- **Use a clear, audible voice**
- **Use friendly and appropriate body language and tone of voice**

FINE TUNINGS

Do I need to do Greeting every single day? What about days when we have no time, when the music teacher is waiting for my class or we're going on a field trip and we need to leave right away?

Greeting, even once the group is well established, is important to do every single day. Once the group is in the habit of forming the Morning Meeting circle, a very quick Greeting can be done in virtually no time. One class at Greenfield Center School has invented a greeting for just such no-time days. It is called "Lefty-Righty" *(Appendix D)* and has become a favorite of the class. Practice it first on a day when you are not rushed to see if it appeals to you.

For the "Tuesday-is-Art-right-away" situation, where the time crunch will be regular, you might suggest that the art teacher join your class for five minutes to be part of Greeting before beginning the art lesson.

Another approach is to do Greeting after your class reconvenes. For example, on field trips teachers sometimes gather students after reaching their destination for a brief check-in and a condensed Meeting with a simple Greeting.

What about the child who just can't speak in front of the group? How can I help him participate in Greeting?

This is not uncommon, particularly with five-year-olds, though some children are painfully shy at older ages as well. As the question implies, it is important to find a way to make sure that these children are part of the routine.

It is helpful to approach this from two angles. First, find a way to help the child participate. Sometimes practicing with the child individually before Meeting, making sure that he knows whom he will greet, helps. Elisabeth Olivera, teacher in a bilingual kindergarten in Holyoke, Massachusetts, suggests that the teacher and student say the words together, with the teacher gradually softening her voice until the child is able to speak on his own.

Second, in your role as interpreter, help the group understand what is going on and how they can be helpful. The explanation should be simple and matter-of-fact: "Terry doesn't want to talk in Meeting yet, but I hope that he will find his words soon. Until he does, you can help by making sure he is greeted and I will help by greeting the next person with him."

This is a wonderful opportunity to validate that it is acceptable, not shameful, for members of the group to struggle sometimes, that we all have our struggles with different activities, and that we can help each other through those struggles with acceptance and encouragement.

My students seem to be getting bored with Greeting.

Variety is important to keep routines from getting stale and this is certainly true of Greeting. There is a fine balance between the comfort and pleasure that predictable, familiar structures bring and the boredom that can pervade the group when there are no changes in format or tempo.

When the mood is boredom, it's time for variation. Introducing new Greetings can happen at any time in the year. Students often come up with clever adaptations to old favorites. I think of the Elbow Rock Greeting *(Appendix D)* which I saw in Kensington School in Springfield, Massachusetts, where fourth grade students had invented an "armshake" in which they extended right arms, bent at the elbow and shook arms rather than hands. There are plenty of Greetings to choose from in *Appendix D*. Teachers often keep a chart with the class repertoire of Greetings posted as a reminder of the possibilities.

It's also important to search for the source of the boredom. Perhaps it is a simple monotony stemming from the same old greeting activities and it's time to introduce some additional choices. Or perhaps the class is turning a developmental corner and the Greetings which were safe and right for your mostly sevens are feeling too narrow for your burgeoning eight-year-olds who crave some sanctioned ways to vent their boisterous side.

I teach in the upper grades and my students usually start out fine with Greeting. However, as the year goes on, they tend to get sloppy and silly. They complain that it's babyish and that they know everyone's names and don't see why they have to keep doing this.

This is not an unusual occurrence, particularly with older children as they get used to Morning Meeting, comfortable with the class, and lax with expectations. When you see children getting sloppy with Greeting, it's time to stop the Meeting. Whispering, nudging, in-jokes, fake smiles, and muffled names are all good reasons to stop a Meeting. When these occur, it's a signal that the class has lost sight of the real purpose behind Greeting and they need some help to get back on track.

A reminder of the purpose behind greetings may be in order. Remind the group that greetings welcome and acknowledge people in the community and that a proper greeting is a vital part of the well-being of the group that day. Emphasize that greeting one another is important work; it is not simply an amusement.

Sometimes sharing a story with the students, such as the one offered earlier about Sue (who never felt acknowledged) or the story of a time when you, as an adult, felt unnoticed helps to remind children of the importance of what they are doing. A discussion about how a sincere versus an insincere greeting really feels may also be helpful. You might ask the children for suggestions of ways to make Greeting work better while also insisting that they greet correctly.

Students always choose their friends to greet first, and the least popular are always left until last to be greeted. How can I address this without embarrassing individuals?

It is important for students to learn to greet all members of the class in a friendly and interested way. We expect students to say "Good morning" to a variety of classmates, not simply their best friends. Almost always, this requires acknowledging and naming this expectation. "If Morning Meeting is a time when we get to know people that we don't usually work or play with, then who might we say 'Good morning' to?" Or, "Today, before we begin Greeting, I want each of us to look around the circle and think of someone we might greet whom we haven't greeted yet this week."

Issues of gender, cliques, and best friends, while present to some degree at most age levels, are developmental milestones of 9–13-year-olds and can manifest themselves with considerable ferocity during those stages. Greeting can help students work on these issues within the safety of teacher-imposed structures.

Some of the behaviors we teach in Morning Meeting, such as making eye contact and smiling at people they don't know, could get my students in real trouble on the streets where they live. How can we ask them to behave one way in school, another way when they go out the door?

Different cultures do have different rules. The culture within our school may be as distant from that which dominates a hundred yards away, as Nigeria is from Finland. It is very important to acknowledge that and to think through what it means for our students. Not only is it possible for them to understand this, it is essential.

Several years ago, I listened to a panel of wise and experienced principals of urban schools discuss this issue. "From a very early age our children must, and do, differentiate and adapt to the different rules that govern their behavior in the several cultures they inhabit every single day—home, streets, school," stated one.

"I talk about the different hats we all wear, and how we sometimes wear the same hat differently in different places," offered another. "In school, we wear our caps with the visor facing front. When we get ready to go out the door to go home, we stop and turn them around. In the hallways of our school you see a stranger, look him in the eyes, smile and say 'Good morning.' In the streets you walk to get home, you see a stranger, you avert your eyes and walk on by."

Sharing

THE ART OF

CARING CONVERSATION

Agreeting has made its way around the circle of fourth-graders and Ms. Scamardella glances at the Sharing Board. "Anita, I notice that you signed up for Sharing today."

"This afternoon," announces Anita, "my Grammy's coming home from the hospital." There is a pause while the other students wait to see if more information is coming. Anita, while not exactly shy, is economical with words. Several children raise their hands. Anita chooses to recognize a boy directly across the circle first. "Reginald."

"I hope she gets well quick," he comments. Anita nods and sends a small smile his way, an acknowledgment of his wish.

Two other hands in the circle are raised. "Sharon," says Anita.

"I didn't know that she was in the hospital. Was she sick for a very long time?"

"They took her in on Sunday," responds Anita. "It was scary because she couldn't eat or anything, her stomach hurt so bad. She even cried when they moved her." Faces around the circle are serious as they receive this detail.

Anita surveys the circle. One classmate raises a hand and Anita calls on her. "Raquel."

"I bet you're glad she can come home," offers Raquel.

Anita nods emphatically. "I am, I really am."

Purposes and Reflections

Sharing follows Greeting in Morning Meeting. It is a structure in which students present news they wish to share and respond to each other by asking questions and offering comments.

Anita's sharing and her classmates' responses reveal a skilled use of verbal communication and an underlying attitude of care. The teacher didn't just get lucky and inherit a class of nine- and ten-year-olds gifted in these ways. She and the teachers of earlier grades in her school teach this behavior and encourage this attitude. They do this, of course, all through the day and all through their curriculum, but one of the times when it is a primary focus is Sharing in Morning Meeting.

Purposes of Sharing

- **Helps develop the skills of caring communication and involvement with one another**
- **Extends the knowing and being known that is essential for the development of community and for individuals' sense of significance**
- **Encourages habits of inquiry and thought important for cognitive growth**
- **Provides practice in speaking to a group in a strong and individual voice**
- **Strengthens vocabulary development and reading success**

Sharing helps develop the skills of caring communication and involvement with one another.

In *The Challenge to Care in Schools,* Nel Noddings offers a clear and instructive exploration of the concept of caring as dependent on the relation between two people. (Noddings 1992, 15–16) She defines a caring relation as a connection or encounter between two human beings—a "carer" and a "cared-for" who must both contribute in certain ways. If either party fails, then there may still be a relation, but it is not a caring relation. The carer must be receptive and attentive to the cared-for and must feel the desire to help the other. The cared-for must receive the act of caring and recognize it by a response.

Sharing in Morning Meeting is the application of this construct, its details translated so that they can be understood and appreciated by five-year-olds and nine-year-olds and fourteen-year-olds. Through modeling, discussion, and practice of their different responsibilities as a sharer and a member of the audience, students develop their understanding of the roles of cared-for and carer and their capacity to assume them.

Eleven-year-old Hallie shares. "Today after school my mother is taking

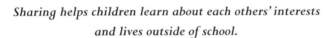

Sharing helps children learn about each others' interests and lives outside of school.

*me to the hospital and I'm gonna' bring cards I made to people there. I'm
ready for questions and comments."*

"Do you want any of us to sign them?"

"Sure. Anybody who wants to."

"I think it's nice of you to do that, to make those cards."

"Thank you."

It is a simple, brief exchange in which both carers and cared-for
are performing fluently. Implicit in the first question is a compliment:
this is a project that sounds so good I'd like to be part of it. In grant-
ing permission, Hallie receives and responds to this offering of care,
just as she does to the next comment, a more direct compliment.

It doesn't always go so smoothly, of course.

"We got a new puppy this weekend," shares kindergartner Tessa.
"I'm ready for questions and comments." Hands shoot up around
the circle. "Allie."

"I have a dog, too, and this morning he threw up on his rug,"
begins Allie, taking a breath as she prepares to launch into her tale.

Her teacher takes advantage of the pause. "Tomorrow when it's
your turn to share you can tell us about your dog. Right now, can
you think of a question or a comment for Tessa about her news?"

Reminded, Allie certainly can. "What does your puppy look
like?" And Sharing is back on track.

Sharing extends the knowing and being known that is essential for the development of community and for individuals' sense of significance.

While Greeting helps everyone know the names of the members
of the classroom community, Sharing builds on that knowledge by
helping children know the people attached to the names. As we
offer information, we learn about each other—whose grandpa just
moved in because he's getting so forgetful, who owns a boa con-
strictor, who loves Matt Christopher books, and who goes to the
YMCA every day after school. Sharing helps build a transition
between home and school.

Sometimes Sharing is structured by a particular topic. "This week we will each share something interesting we learned from the biographies we are reading," assigns the teacher, or "This week Sharing will be about something you made." Although the Sharing topic is focused, sharers reveal unique and individual information nonetheless.

Often the revelations help establish a common ground between students which is carried beyond the Meeting. Consulting Teacher Marlynn Clayton, skilled teacher of young children, notes that she frequently helps children spot the connection and extend it. "There isn't time for more comments in Sharing, but maybe the three of you could have lunch together and talk more about your baseball card collections," she might suggest.

This kind of gentle guidance helps students move beyond their existing circle of friends. Left to our own devices, we often spend time with those whom we are most comfortable, those most "like us," which limits our growth. Sharing allows students to begin with a common interest, a starting place from which to learn about differences as well as similarities. The richest communication requires both acknowledgment of common ground and ability to explore differences in perspective and ideas.

Sharing which lets every member of the community hear and be heard demands an engagement that stretches our understanding and rewards us all.

Sharing encourages habits of inquiry and thought important for cognitive growth.

The research of many respected educational theorists, including Piaget and Vygotsky, has examined and documented the relationship between social context and cognitive development. (Rogoff 1990, 192) Though Piaget and Vygotsky each describe different models for the ways in which social interaction influences cognitive development, both recognize the importance of developing the following skills:

- Stating one's thoughts with clarity
- Listening actively and forming questions which clarify
- Seeing things from another's perspective

Sharing in Morning Meeting spurs children's cognitive growth because these important cognitive skills are embedded in the format for presentation and response and are nourished by their practice.

Stating one's thoughts with clarity

In order to present a piece of news to classmates, students must be able to craft a comprehensible narration and deliver it. If it is not clear, the feedback will be immediate.

"Wait a minute. I'm confused. Was it your brother or your father who forgot to pick you up last night?" Todd asks his classmate, Michael, after a rambling and confused story. It is a genuine question; Todd wants to understand and respond to Michael's experience.

Listening actively and forming questions which clarify

Active listening is motivated by the expectation that each student's job is to formulate a question that elicits more information or to make a comment that shows interest in the news presented or concern for the sharer. When students accept these responsibilities, they listen carefully and remember well, habits important for every learner.

To further promote good listening, particularly in earlier grades, teachers will sometimes ask questions at the end of Sharing which test the group's ability to recall details. "Who can remember the name of Leanne's turtle?" "What was the name of the fruit Marisa brought in?"

Seeing things from another's perspective

Sheldon Berman, co-founder of Educators for Social Responsibility, stated in a recent address that taking another's perspective "is the linchpin in the development of social consciousness. How can we get beyond ourselves, know what's going on for another person? That's where social responsibility begins." (Berman 1998)

Comments which respond to Sharing require seeing things from another's perspective. Commenting well entails understanding another person's situation, feelings, and motives. Whether the sharing is about something momentous or the everyday stuff of our lives, responding well requires stepping outside our own vantage point to try and imagine how another person feels or regards something.

"I bet you feel really happy that you can get your cast taken off tomorrow."

"I think the way you made the orange and the red blur together in your painting really looks like fire."

"I hope your cat will be all right."

All are statements informed by empathy, by that ability to "get beyond ourselves" which Berman notes. They are comments which say "I listened to you. I care about how you feel."

Sharing provides practice in speaking to a group in a strong and individual voice.

Many adults share a deep apprehension, ranging from nervousness to utter terror, at the thought of speaking to a group. In my own school experience, we spoke to a group only in formal and artificial situations, seldom on anything we really knew about or of deep interest to us. Instead, we were assigned to do "Oral Reports" on designated topics, reports that were thinly disguised paraphrases of encyclopedia passages. Grades were correlated to the length of time we spoke, rather than the content. It took at least five horrifying minutes to get an "A" in seventh grade English class. Mumbling helped disguise the fact that we couldn't pronounce a third of the words we had painstakingly copied.

How blessedly different Sharing is! First of all, the material has intrinsic interest and students can make choices even within structured topics. A student assigned to share news "that shows courage" has many choices. Will she share about her seventy-two-year-old grandmother, always terrified of the water, who is now bravely taking beginner's swimming lessons? Or will she share a story she saw on television's evening news about firefighters who rescued three people from a downtown apartment fire last night?

Also, one of our jobs as sharer is to keep our presentation brief and understandable rather than padding it to stretch it out. When others are listening and want to respond, they will not allow us to mumble or to speak in those rapid, inaudible monotones which were the style in my seventh-grade class. The chance to practice is frequent, brief, informal (yet structured), and unjudged by letter grades.

Sharing strengthens vocabulary development and reading success.

The Home-School Study of Language and Literacy Development is a longitudinal study investigating the links between early oral language development of children and their literacy success in elementary and middle school. One of their findings is that opportunities for children to participate in "interesting conversations with adults" are strongly related to children's reading success in school. The study found that it is important for children to engage regularly in "conversation that goes beyond the here and now, and which relies on language to convey images and information about other times and places. A girl describing a recent trip to the zoo over dinner, for example, would rely on her decontextualized language skills to describe what she had seen." (Lynn 1997, 2) This is exactly the kind of conversation that takes place during Sharing.

As students work at expressing themselves and understanding others through conversation, the process is filled with opportunities for vocabulary enrichment. In the context of the "real" conversations in Sharing, teachers may use words and terms that may be unfamiliar to students and correct students' misunderstandings of vocabulary.

Consider this scene from a third grade classroom I visited recently. It was Regina's turn to share.

"On Saturday I went to Adventure World with my uncle. I went swimming there and I drowned," states Regina.

Her classmates are full of questions about her trip. The first questions seek to establish the logistics of her trip.

"What parts of Adventure World did you go to?"

"How long did it take to get there?"

"Was there traffic?"

Then comes a question that moves past the details to the core of her sharing. "Was it scary when you drowned?"

Wide-eyed and solemn, Regina nods emphatically. "It was really scary."

Her teacher has listened and observed intently during these exchanges. She notices that all of the children understand Regina's news and they all share the same misunderstanding.

"Regina," she asks, "when you said that you drowned, did you mean that you had trouble swimming in the water?"

Regina nods, yes, that's what she meant. An impromptu vocabulary lesson follows, a thread picked up from the fabric of Regina's sharing, and woven seamlessly into the classroom circle.

"Drowned is connected to having trouble in the water," affirms the teacher, "but it means that you had so much trouble that you died from not being able to get above the water to breathe."

The class listens intently. There is no embarrassment attached to the mistake; they are glad to receive this information, given crisply and matter-of-factly. It extends their ability to describe their own experiences and to interpret the experiences of others accurately in both oral and written communications.

Highlights of Sharing

- Provides an arena for students to share news
- Helps students develop the ability to gauge the appropriateness of sharing various kinds of news with different audiences
- Allows students to practice framing constructive, purposeful questions
- Helps students develop a repertoire of responses to different kinds of news
- Develops good oral communication skills—both presentation skills and listening skills
- Lets students learn information about each other
- Enhances vocabulary development and reading success
- Offers practice in speaking to a group
- Gives practice in considering others' perspectives, developing empathy and social consciousness
- Empowers students by letting them run their sharing

GETTING STARTED

Introduce Sharing

Sharing is usually the last component of Morning Meeting to be introduced, after Greeting, Group Activity, and News and Announcements have been introduced and established. (See *Fine Tunings* section of the chapter, "Morning Meeting: An Overview," for a review of the issues involved in the order of components.)

Introduce Sharing by explaining its purpose and structure. "One of the purposes of Morning Meeting is to help us get to know each other better. Each day in our Morning Meeting there will be a time for some of us to share news about things in our lives with the class. Everyone will get a chance to share, though usually not every day."

In this introduction, brainstorm with children appropriate things to share, making sure that events and information are included, not just objects. Ideas will vary with different ages, of course. This introductory session is a time to generate ideas with a broad scope of possible topics; unless an idea for something to share is conspicuously inappropriate, it is not a time to limit or refine notions about Sharing. That will evolve as Sharing is practiced.

Discuss and model the "jobs" of the sharer.

The "jobs" of the sharer include using a voice that is strong and clear and sharing news which is brief and focused. "I'm going to share," begins the teacher, "about something that I saw while driving to school this morning. I had to stop and wait because twelve wild turkeys were in the middle of the road, just milling around. They didn't seem to even notice my car." He calls upon his students to note that his voice is strong and clear and his news brief and focused and reminds them to think about those "jobs" when it is their turn to share.

When your students are preparing for their first sharings early in the year, you may want to assign each sharer a partner who will listen to the sharing ahead of time and give feedback based on the defined "jobs" of the sharer.

- Did the sharer use a strong voice?

- Was the news short and clear?

Children sometimes need help focusing their sharing. It is often hard for them to select the most important things, rather than tell everything. "Tell one important part of your visit to the zoo," can be helpful. Some teachers, particularly of younger children or of children who want to tell "breakfast-to-bed" stories, use a "two sentence rule" as a sharing guideline. Sometimes, however, when the speaker just can't stop rambling, the teacher must interrupt.

Children listen more carefully to the sharing when they
are expected to formulate good questions and comments.

"You've told us lots of interesting things about your team, Sara. Let's see if there are questions."

Discuss and model good questions and comments.

Audience members have two important jobs. First, they must listen carefully to the sharer. Second, they must respond with respectful, caring questions and comments.

Good questions

What is a good question? Good questions show a genuine interest in the sharer and her news. They can inquire about the factual or emotional content of a sharing and get information which extends understanding about what has been shared. Sometimes a question clarifies information. Good questions are often open-ended, requiring more than just a yes or no response from the sharer.

Good questions reflect the spirit of Sharing—the sharer is acknowledged, noticed, and encouraged. What might be a wonderful question in a debate club—challenging and argumentative, designed to exhibit the knowledge of the questioner—is an unacceptable question in Sharing.

Good questioning skills can be practiced quite deliberately. After sharing about her turkey sighting, the teacher says to her class, "Today we're going to practice asking good questions. Your questions might ask about something that you didn't understand. They might ask for more information about what I told you or they might ask how I felt about it."

"How big were the turkeys?"

"What did they look like?"

"Were you worried that you might hit one?"

"Why do you think they were in the road?"

"How did you get them to move out of the road?"

A specific kind of question-asking skill may be isolated and practiced, also. "Today I want each person to think of a question about my sharing that cannot be answered by just yes or no."

Good comments

Good comments notice and appreciate elements of the sharing and keep the focus on the sharer. Laura has brought a photo of her new puppy to share. Interest is high among her classmates; almost every one has a hand raised. The questions asked are full of real interest and a full picture of this puppy emerges from Laura's answers. It's a girl, she sleeps a lot, eats a lot, and in between she likes to chew things, sometimes things she's not supposed to. The vet thinks she will get to be at least seventy-five pounds and Laura got her from somebody her dad works with whose dog had puppies and needed to find homes for them.

The comments, however, consist entirely of other pet owners' stories. Each one is a variation on the theme of "When I got my dog (hamster, kitten) . . ." While this would be lovely lunch table conversation, the focus moving from person to person but related to a central topic, it does not fit the guidelines for Sharing comments. A lesson on comments that focus upon the sharer is in order and the teacher decides to capitalize on the eager involvement of the class, directing their interest back to Laura's story.

"I want everyone in the circle to think of a comment that speaks about Laura's news. You might say something that you notice or you might think about how she seems to feel about getting her puppy and comment about that." There is a thoughtful silence as the children sift their ideas through the filters their teacher has named. Slowly the hands go back up.

"I think your puppy looks really sweet."

"I noticed how one ear stands up and one ear doesn't in your picture. I think that's really cute."

"I hope your puppy doesn't chew any more of your shoes."

"I think it's really nice that you took a puppy that might not have had a home otherwise."

"I bet you're really happy to have a puppy."

"Five comments and every one of them was directly connected to Laura's news about her puppy. You really paid attention to Laura," recognizes the teacher.

Set up a system which gives everyone the chance to share.

Most teachers find it helpful to have a sign-up system which ensures that each child is a sharer at least once a week. Children can sign up to share the day before Meeting or that same morning. Another way is to assign each child a regular day for sharing. Limiting the number of questions and comments each sharer can accept can help to keep Sharing moving and feeling equitable.

Make sure to give children the responsibility to conduct their sharing.

Let the sharer call on people who have questions and comments. As teachers, we often lead or chair discussions and slide easily into this unacceptable role during Sharing. Try to be aware of this habit and work on changing to a less directive approach. Sharing will be much more meaningful if children feel a sense of ownership and responsibility for conducting their sharing.

Focus the flow and type of sharing and responses as necessary.
There will be many times when you need to direct the flow
because questions and comments are being offered by the same
students or certain sharings elicit little response. It is important to
address these issues directly, enabling students to think about and
practice the skills of conversation involved. It may be time for a
refresher course in good questioning or commenting, or a review
of the sharer's job and some modeling. This differs from earlier
modeling because it focuses on a particular aspect of Sharing skills
in response to a problem you observe.

Begin by naming what you see as the problem. "I notice," you
might say at the next day's Meeting, "that, even though there has
been some really interesting sharing, lots of us aren't thinking of
questions or comments." Or, "I've been noticing that sometimes,
when we share, we tell so many details that the audience has a really
hard job thinking of anything important to ask."

Then structure an exercise, offering yourself as model, that will
address what you have named.

"Listen to my sharing and notice all the facts I've told you. Last night

Most teachers find it helpful to have a sign-up system which ensures
that each child is a sharer at least once a week.

I went to see a play my daughter was in.What facts did you hear?"
"You went to a play."
"Your daughter was in it."
"It was last night."
"What didn't I tell you that you might want to know?"
"What was the name of the play?"
"Was it funny or serious?"
"What was the name of the character your daughter played?"
"Did your daughter remember all her lines?"
"Was it a really long play?" This from Mark, who hates to sit still.
"Where was it? A fancy theater?"

"Wow. You thought of five questions based on a sharing that only told you three facts,"I note."The rest of this week I want our sharers to make sure they tell only a couple of important facts in their sharing, and I want the audience to pay attention to what else it would be interesting to find out."

Don't be afraid to intervene in your role as "guide."

Teachers guide students' participation in the art of caring conversation. "Guided participation," says psychologist Barbara Rogoff, "involves children and their caregivers and companions in the collaborative processes of (1) building bridges from children's present understanding and skills to reach new understanding and skills, and (2) arranging and structuring children's participation in activities, with dynamic shifts over development in children's responsibilities." (Rogoff 1990, 8)

We all participate in conversations throughout the day. School days, for children, should be, and generally are, full of opportunities for conversations. The guided participation of Sharing at Morning Meeting, however, has a number of important distinctions from the conversational participation at the water cooler or the sand table. The teacher's role as a guide and the structures of Sharing enable verbal interactions and responses that children may not yet be capable of independently.

This situation came to life for me in a visit to Cynthia Donnelly's first grade classroom in Springfield, Massachusetts.

It was December, only a few days before the holiday vacation and these six-year-olds were spilling over with the excitement of the season. Cynthia's understanding of her class and her years of experience were called upon frequently to keep them focused at Morning Meeting.

A hasty version of Speed Ball Greeting had left several children ungreeted, to which Cynthia had responded, "OK, that was just a test run. Now we'll try it again, being speedy and remembering everybody." What a gracious and adept way to demand that they do it right. And do it right they did, beating their prior record of fifty-one seconds, with everyone included.

"Nice job, class," affirmed Cynthia. "Today, Anthony will share first."

Anthony leaned forward eagerly and his words flew out fast and excited. "My grandma's coming from Italy to visit me!"

"He already told us that!" blurted Adam. It was a thoroughly six-year-old retort, brash and impulsive, tinged with righteous indignation at having to hear something twice. It was really not meant to be unkind, though it fell with a cruel thud upon the enthusiastic Anthony. Adam—and a crestfallen Anthony—along with their nineteen classmates, looked to their teacher for a ruling.

But their teacher didn't offer them one. Instead she offered them a question. It was a question that masterfully sidestepped the issue of whether the news had or hadn't been offered before and pointed her students toward a more important issue. "If Anthony already told us his grandma was coming, why might he tell us again? What would make a person repeat news?"

Several ideas were ventured. "I say things twice when I'm really excited!"

"Maybe Anthony's got more to tell than when he told it the first time."

"Probably 'cause it's really important news to you."

Cynthia nodded, receiving these suggestions thoughtfully, before handing the reins back to Anthony. "OK, Anthony, you can choose people for questions and comments." Questions abounded:

"How long since you saw her?"

"When's she coming?"

"Is she gonna bring you a present from Italy?"

Cynthia's hand is up in the air. "Maybe, Anthony, your grandma could come to school with you."

Without the guidance of their teacher, it is unlikely that a group of six-year-olds could have moved beyond their concern about the detail of Adam's observation into a contemplation based upon empathy for Anthony. It is more likely that their diversion into "who said what when" would have prevented them from responding to Anthony's news at all.

This is not to suggest that Cynthia, in the thirty seconds in which she responded to the situation, considered the theoretical foundation and the probable effects of her actions, consciously constructing an opportunity for "guided participation." Construct it she did, however, in a moment infused by a remarkable mix of teacherly instinct and expertise.

The structures and guided aspect of Sharing also allow freedom to fumble and stumble as we learn. Cynthia's intervention and response to Adam's comment let her whole class know that the important thing was to think about Anthony and to respond to his news in a caring way. By not engaging directly with Adam or with the substance of his accusation—whether Anthony had or hadn't shared this already—she let them know that it was not a helpful comment. But she did this in a way that did not highlight Adam or his blunder.

Adam stood corrected, but gently and quickly. In order to learn from our mistakes, the feedback must be clear enough so that we understand what we must try to do differently next time, but not so sharp that we recoil in embarrassment. When our humiliation is large or when we are mired in our own awkwardness with no hand extended to pull us out, we learn defensiveness or avoidance instead of a more positive form of engagement.

Because Sharing is a whole class activity, there is the potential for all to learn from each interaction. Cynthia invited the whole class to help solve the puzzle of why a person might share old news. In this structure and under her guidance, the discovery was not limited to the two boys directly involved, but became a spontaneous, whole-class lesson in understanding and motivation.

**As the class becomes familiar with the basic format of
Sharing, give structure to the content as needed.**

Sometimes teachers need to take an active role in directing the
content of Sharing. I have a painful memory of substituting in a fifth
and sixth grade classroom where I did not know the students and
their demographics well. It was the day after February vacation and
the first three sharings involved the details of expensive ski vaca-
tions—the depth of the powder, the temperature in Colorado, the
hot springs. Trying desperately to figure out how to redirect this
mostly unintentional cruelty, I watched the expressions on the
faces of the children who had spent their week at home watching
younger siblings or going to the local YMCA program.

Obviously we don't want to stifle children from sharing about
special opportunities that come their way. But we do want our
classrooms to be places where economic distinctions are not used
to oppress. One way we can address this within the context of
Sharing is by helping students to identify and share about activities
and news which are non-material—which don't involve things or
special opportunities based on economics. A post-vacation week
Sharing topic might be about someone you spent time with during
vacation, for example.

A variation of the "Luxury Vacation" sharing that shows up in
classes of younger children is the "Bring and Brag" syndrome. Many
teachers avoid this by a general "No toys for sharing" rule.
Recognizing, however, that sometimes it is important to have a
chance to share a special toy, many teachers define a category—
Category Sharing—to allow those opportunities while providing
some focus which keeps the emphasis away from the completely
materialistic. One week might be "Bring Your Favorite Stuffie
Week" or "Bring A Toy You Made Week."

Sometimes teachers use categories simply to give children ideas
about different kinds of sharing, such as news about "Grandparents"
or "Something You Found in Nature." With older children, sharing
focused upon current events is often very successful.

Help students distinguish between news appropriate for classroom sharing and news to be shared just with the teacher.

For the purposes of Morning Meeting, there are two overall categories of news—Community News and Private Family News. Community News is news that is appropriate for the classroom community to hear and Private Family News is news that is not appropriate for sharing with the whole class. This might be news that is confidential from a legal or ethical viewpoint. It might involve details a child has overheard about a court case a family member is involved in or it might involve a sticky family situation (such as a divorce or family dispute) about which a child has enormous emotion but little information or understanding.

Let children know that they can tell you, their teacher, this kind of news, but not the whole class. Making this distinction not only protects the child and the family but also protects the rest of the class from access to information that is beyond their capacity to cope with or understand.

Reassure children that sometimes it's hard to decide whether certain news is suitable for group sharing. If they ever have something which feels like it could be Private Family News, they should always "try out" their sharing with you first to help make this judgment.

Prepare students to handle the sharing of Serious News.

Community News can be light, humorous, or matter-of-fact. It may also be sad and painful or worrisome. When the classroom climate is safe and comfortable, both kinds of news can be offered and received with care and respect.

Younger children tend to blurt out what they need to say when they need to say it. With the help of their teacher, however, they are very able to recognize that some news is serious and demands a different kind of response than other, lighter news. As teachers, we can model a response: "I'm sorry to hear that your dad is in the hospital."

Older children can be more deliberate about the sharing of

*Sharing offers opportunities for children to develop
a repertoire of responses to different kinds of news.*

serious news. Some teachers of older children introduce labels for the two types of Community News—Newsy News and Serious News, for example. When a class first begins using the format of Sharing, most news offered naturally tends to be Newsy News. When class members are at ease with the structures of sharing, questions, and comments, and when they trust each other to respond easily and respectfully to Newsy News, you might inform the group that they are ready to add Serious News.

Emphasize that the children should always bring Serious News to you first and you will determine whether it's appropriate to share with the group. In some cases, you may need to help a child modify the Serious News in order to make it appropriate; in other cases, you may need to explain to a child that the news is not suitable to share with the class. Let parents know ahead of time that you will be introducing Serious News and that you will be carefully filtering any Serious News the children bring for Sharing.

Through discussion and brainstorming, help the children sort and categorize their news. What are some examples of Newsy

News? Serious News? It is also helpful to generate ideas for constructive responses to different kinds of news. If someone shares
something sad, what can we say to let them know that we listened
well and that we care how they feel?

These are not skills commonly taught. Recently, I saw a book
titled *How to Say It,* offering "ready-to-use letters to suit every personal or professional occasion no matter what the situation." The
market for such books indicates that, even as well-intentioned
adults, we struggle to know what the "right" words are. Too often,
our awkwardness and discomfort can cause us to avoid acknowledging another's pain or offering our help. The practice provided
by responding to news in Sharing can help us feel more competent
at navigating these situations.

Sharing Responsibilities

In implementing and assessing Sharing, keep the following general
responsibilities in mind.

Teachers' responsibilities

- Set up systems for signing up and for the number
  of questions and comments allowed
- Act as facilitator and timekeeper, keeping the
  process moving
- Model good oral communication skills
- Model appropriate language for questions and
  comments
- Help students keep the focus upon the sharer
- Screen out sharing which is inappropriate for the
  group

Students' responsibilities

- Choose news that is appropriate to share with the
  group

- **Organize their ideas and keep their sharing brief**
- **Wait their turn to share**
- **Place any objects they need in the designated Sharing place**
- **Listen attentively to others' sharing**
- **Ask questions and make comments which show interest, respect, and caring**
- **Stay focused upon the sharer**

FINE TUNINGS

What should I do when a child starts telling about something that's really inappropriate for Sharing time?

Sometimes children are honestly not sure what category some news falls into and may begin sharing a piece of news that feels inappropriate to you. Perhaps it is a piece of family news that isn't for public consumption; or perhaps it is news that is too scary for the class to handle. Occasionally children manipulate attention by using shocking or disturbing revelations.

The mother of seven-year-old Katie is a reporter and is privy to many details of a particularly gory local murder. Though you know that she tries to protect Katie from hearing more than she needs to, Katie's powers of hearing and overhearing are highly developed and she specializes in eavesdropping on phone calls and conversations that are saved for after her bedtime.

"There's a lot of stuff about the body of that guy," she begins her sharing one day, "stuff that the police aren't telling people." Your "Appropriateness Detector" is beeping loudly. Intervene without over-reacting and move on. "Katie, I'd like you to hold onto the rest of your sharing until I can talk with you about it later. I'm not sure that it is news for our whole class to hear."

Listen to Katie as soon as possible after Meeting ends and let her know whether her news is suitable for the classroom audience or should be saved for you. In a case such as this one, a phone call to the parent is also in order.

What should I do when students don't speak loudly enough for others to hear them? Or when they can't understand a particular child? Should I repeat that child's words?

Though this is a situation calling for individual judgment, a general guideline is to resist "voice-overs." Allow sharers to speak for themselves unless there are severe speech problems or some other issue clearly creating communication difficulties. Make sure students know and use courteous ways of telling a child that they didn't hear or understand something that was said. This is important feedback for speakers, and it is necessary for the conversation to continue.

Is it all right for me to ask questions and make comments or should I leave that to the other students?

It is definitely all right for you to ask questions and offer comments. In fact, it is vital for students to see that you find their news interesting and that you care about how things are going for them. It's also a good opportunity to model questions and comments in an unobtrusive way.

However, it's best to allow students to respond first and be sure not to respond to every single sharing. If you do, the message is that an exchange isn't really valid until the teacher has spoken.

I know I should discourage responses that involve the responder's experiences rather than focusing on the sharer—comments like "I have a dog, too, and . . ." But sometimes it seems like those responses are honest attempts at connection and empathy, not simple egocentrism. Is it ever OK to allow such comments?

This questions involves an important distinction, a judgment call we must make as we guide Sharing. Is the intention of the response to highlight a connection with the sharer and acknowledge a bond revealed by the sharing? Or is the intention to divert the focus from the sharer to the responder and his or her news?

Like many distinctions, this is not always clear and tidy. What begins as an acknowledgment of connection can unintentionally slide quickly into one's own sharing. When that happens, the teacher needs to stop the commenting child with a respectful reminder, "That sounds like some interesting sharing about you, Chris. You could share it tomorrow when it is your turn. Now you can ask Bruce a question or make a comment about his sharing."

The goal is to help children respond to another's experience without bringing it back to themselves. Some teachers give students a specific phrase to help them frame this kind of response, a phrase which lets them draw upon their own genuine connections while remembering their job of keeping the focus on the sharer. "I have a connection to you, Chris, because we have a car like that. Maybe we can talk about it later."

I often run into problems with the logistics of children bringing in objects to share. Children can't find the object when it's their turn to share. Everyone in the circle wants a chance to touch the object. Arguments occur over how classmates handle the object. With so much attention focused on the object itself, how can I keep the child's sharing from getting lost in the shuffle?

The sharing of objects can create lots of problems in addition to the "Bring and Brag" syndrome previously discussed. There are a variety of strategies you may want to use if you are going to have children bring in objects for Sharing. One is to designate a "Show Shelf" or "Sharing Basket" in your room. When children bring in an object for Sharing, they leave it in this spot where others are able to view it but not touch it.

Once the object is shared, it's put back on the shelf until the end of the day. If the sharer wants children to handle the object later in the day, he/she can explain and demonstrate during Sharing how the object should be handled. Finally, as a general

*Having a designated shelf for any objects brought in
for Sharing can alleviate many problems.*

rule, don't allow objects to be passed around the circle. It usually takes a very long time during which the focus is shifted from the sharer to the object itself.

There are lots of questions in response to sharings in my classroom, but seldom any comments. Why is that and what can I do?

The situation you name is quite common in classrooms. Chip Wood, author and teacher of both children and adults, sees a difference between questions and comments that helps explain it. He notes that question-asking is essentially egocentric; questions usually arise from information that you wish for yourself. Commenting, by contrast, requires empathy, the ability to take another's perspective and think about what he or she needs in order to feel cared for at that moment. Finding language to empathize can be challenging and may feel risky.

It's important to help your class understand the difference between questions and comments, and to provide low-risk opportunities to practice making comments. Try offering news of your own as material upon which to practice: "This morning I am going to share about something that happened to me on the way to school and I want only comments—not questions, but comments—from the audience. On the way in to school today I dropped all my papers in a puddle in our parking lot. I'm ready for comments."

Choose a common situation with which all students can identify. We need to learn to respond to the everyday pleasures and irritations as well as the moments of high drama which comprise our lives. With practice, we can build our vocabulary for caregiving and we can achieve a comfort level that lets us use it.

Group Activity

L et's recite our class poem,"
announces the teacher and nineteen seven- and eight-year-old voices
dutifully offer up a sing-song rendition of the October stanza from
Maurice Sendak's poem "Chicken Soup with Rice." (Sendak 1962)

> *In October*
> *I'll be host*
> *to witches, goblins*
> *and a ghost.*
> *I'll serve them*
> *chicken soup*
> *on toast.*
> *Whoopy once*
> *whoopy twice*
> *whoopy chicken soup*
> *with rice.*

"We've got the words down," says their teacher, "and now we're
going to do it in our scary voices. Take a minute and think about
how you can make your voice sound scary."

Eyes twinkle and smiles flicker on their faces as the second-graders ponder and await their teacher's signal to begin. In a dramatic transformation from their earlier version, the young voices have grown deep and slow and mysterious. As they finish, the smiles that had flickered earlier erupt into full-fledged grins and chuckles. They revel in the sound of their collective voice.

"Mmmm . . . very nice. Let's think about reciting that at next week's All-School Meeting," compliments their teacher.

Down the hall the first graders are singing the Friends' Song. "Friends, friends, one, two, three. All my friends are here with me. You're my friend . . ." They already know it in English, Spanish, and French. Today they will learn how to perform it in sign language.

On the second floor, the fifth-graders are intent on guessing a

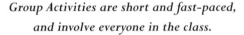

Group Activities are short and fast-paced,
and involve everyone in the class.

category made up by their classmate, Caleb, who is doling out indirect clues in a game called Aunt Minerva *(See Appendix E).*

"Aunt Minerva likes Florida but doesn't like Alaska," announces Caleb.

No responses.

Caleb tries again. "Aunt Minerva likes heavy down quilts but doesn't like thin sheets."

Two hands shoot up and Caleb calls on Sonya.

"Aunt Minerva likes soup but doesn't like ice cream?" ventures Sonya, her voice making the statement a question.

"That's true," nods Caleb.

"Danny?" Danny has retracted his hand after hearing Sonya's contribution. "Nope, I'm not ready yet."

After a few more guesses about Aunt Minerva's preferences, half the hands in the circle are raised, and Mr. Bergstrom, the teacher, spots a good stopping place. All have grappled with the process of set-making but the "who-hasn't-got-it-yet" syndrome hasn't yet set in.

"Pick a guesser, Caleb," Mr. Bergstrom directs, and Caleb points to Josie.

"Is it hot and cold?" she asks.

Caleb's smile and nod confirms it.

Purposes and Reflections

As the above vignettes illustrate, Group Activities are short, fast-paced activities involving everyone in the class. Some activities have clear academic skill-building components and may tie in to current topics in the curriculum; other activities appear "just for fun" and offer practice in more generalized skills like listening, following directions, exercising self-control, or rolling the ball gently.

Purposes of Group Activity

- **Contributes to the sense of community culture by building a class repertoire of common material— songs, games, chants, and poems**
- **Fosters active and engaged participation**
- **Heightens the class's sense of group identity**
- **Encourages cooperation and inclusion**

You may want to browse through *Appendix E* before continuing. It lists a wide variety of Group Activities, some of which are referred to by name in the text.

Group Activity contributes to the sense of community culture by building a class repertoire of common material— songs, games, chants, and poems.

It's clean-up time and Shawna and Leo are methodically taking the large wooden unit blocks from their skyscraper and stacking them neatly on the appointed shelf. "Whoopy once, whoopy twice," chants Leo under his breath as he leans from the pile of blocks to the shelf, lost in his rhythm of stack and tidy and lean again. Shawna, done with the dismantling of their creation, moves closer to help him. "Whoopy chicken soup with rice," she chimes in. Her voice layers over her companion's as neatly as the blocks they stack on the shelf.

The chants and songs, games and story lines that are introduced during Group Activity time are a common and crucial currency in the classroom community. They contribute to a shared archive from which children can draw when they are riding the bus together on a field trip, in a companionable clean-up moment, or at the snack table. We feel a sense of belonging, comfort, and acceptance when we recognize a familiar melody, when we are invited into a game and realize that we know the rules, when someone refers to a funny story and we find that we know that story, too. We are at home in this place, with these people.

Sometimes the common learning provides us with a way to affirm our group identity within a larger community. When the second grade stands before the rest of the school and intones their ghosts and goblins stanza of "Chicken Soup," it is a wonderful declaration of their solidarity. As they stand together and speak with one voice to the audience, they are clearly a cohesive group.

Group Activity fosters active and engaged participation.

Good choices for Group Activities are active rather than passive and require everyone's participation. They can be a great "wake-up call" at the outset of the day because they demand that each of us pay attention and contribute. It's not easy to snooze through a fast-paced game of Ra-de-o or Zoom or to let your attention wander when it will be your turn soon to think up an equation for today's date, and the first six people have used up the obvious number statements.

For today's Group Activity, these children learn hand games they will later use when there is "waiting time" in the classroom.

Joining in the tempo of the Group Activity can help students find a productive pace for moving into the rest of the day. We all have different rhythms and gaits, and our differences bring richness to the group of which we are a part. But we also have our days when something in our pace is "off." We may arrive at school distracted, replaying a conflict at the breakfast table in our head. We may arrive speedy and frazzled, moving at top speed to compensate for oversleeping, needing help to change gears and settle down. Joining a group activity, moving in unison, can sometimes help us find our most comfortable stride.

Group Activity heightens a class's sense of group identity.

Being part of a whole group activity builds cohesiveness and deepens individuals' sense of responsibility as group members.

In *Promoting Social and Emotional Learning,* an anecdote describes how an "exemplary" high school teacher uses games as warm-up activities. One day the game was group juggling—each student receiving a ball from a specific person and tossing it to another specific person. As the game progressed and more balls were added, concentration increased and laughter erupted frequently. When discussing the game afterwards, students mentioned that having a group goal led to a sense of responsibility—everyone had to be fully alert to achieve the group goal. The laughter added to the sense of closeness among students. (Elias et al. 1997, 54)

The universal human need to have fun was discussed in the chapter, "Morning Meeting: An Overview." Group Activities—whether they involve seeing how fast a hand squeeze can travel all around the circle or how many words can be formed from the word "December"—are often fun. They evoke smiles and laughter and a sense of satisfaction. They are also productive and teach skills useful in academic learning.

This doesn't necessarily mean that Group Activities are always games or activities we usually think of as "fun." The activities must demand that the group pull together and that all members are involved, but they might be a class recitation of a poem or a choral reading, daily math rituals, or group story writing.

Group Activity encourages cooperation and inclusion.

Good Group Activities allow all members to take part. Although some students will excel in certain activities, some in others, each Group Activity must be accessible to all. A teacher's knowledge of her class will guide the choice of activities. They shouldn't all feel easy—a sure route to complaints of "Boring." But neither should activities be ones in which only a couple of "gifted" students can feel successful, for this will be demoralizing and isolating for others in the group. Celebrating individual talents and achievements is definitely healthy in a classroom, but Group Activity is not the place for it.

Successful activities often stretch and challenge the group. They work well when those stretches and challenges are deliberate choices on the teacher's part and are introduced when the group is ready to take on a challenge which will feel safe for the group and the individuals. Helping the class to notice their increasing proficiency with a challenging activity affirms the role of practice and effort in learning.

I once heard a group of fifth graders groan, "We'll never be able to say this," upon a first read-through of *The Gettysburg Address*. "We can't even pronounce half these words." And they were right. They couldn't pronounce them. Yet two weeks later, after intensive coaching and many practice sessions, these fifth-graders could do more than pronounce. They proclaimed—with resonant voices and nary a stumble.

"Remember how two weeks ago you were never going to be able to recite this?" reminded their teacher. This was such an important lesson: that what seems insurmountable at first can indeed be surmounted with effort and support. Learning this lesson will serve these students well as they go on to confront the mysterious equations algebra offers, the unfamiliar constructions of a Shakespearean line or the booklet of directions for installing the garage door opener.

Although Group Activities should be cooperative, not competitive, in nature, it is sometimes fun for the group to "compete" against itself. Can they beat their previous time at Electricity, a game in which they must work together to pass a hand squeeze around the circle as quickly as possible? Can they come up with more equations for 23 on the 23rd of this month than they could on the 23rd of last month? Many classes enjoy keeping a log of their best times for various activities. But this kind of competition is best used sparingly, so that the emphasis remains on the activity rather than the contest.

Highlights of Group Activity

- Provides a way for all class members to learn a common set of songs, chants, games, poems, etc.
- Lets the group experience working together to produce an outcome impossible as individuals or a small group
- Demands cooperation
- Encourages inclusion
- Fosters active and engaged participation
- Allows students to see each others' differing strengths
- Provides experience in having fun together as a group
- Gives an opportunity to reinforce and extend social and academic skills
- Allows for the integration and practice of curriculum content

GETTING STARTED

Introduce Group Activity, modeling appropriate behaviors.

Explain that this is a time within Morning Meeting when the whole group will do an activity together. In whatever language is appropriate and respectful to the age group, note that it will be important in these activities for each person to take good care of herself or himself, as well as taking care of other people in the group.

Choosing a couple of aspects which are important to the activity for the day, model constructive behaviors related to those aspects. Eventually, you will find it helpful to model the following:

- Voice level

- Physical controls

- Taking turns

- Making mistakes

- Problem-solving

- Cooperative play

"Eventually" is a key word here. Opportunities to model and discuss how activities are going will happen throughout the year. Carefully choose relatively fail-safe activities at the outset so that the group experiences success without the need for extensive preparation. It is better to model one element at a time, specifically and thoroughly, than to try to conduct an exhaustive (and exhausting!) Grand Tour of constructive activity behaviors.

"Today we are going to play a fast and in-control game of Speed Ball," Mr. Coughlin tells his first grade class. "*I'm going to throw the ball to Willy. Watch me and tell me what makes it both fast and in-control."* He throws it low and carefully and Willy catches it easily.

"What did you notice?"

"You didn't throw it over his head," volunteers Zeke.

"That's right. And where did I aim it?"

"At his belly." Mr. Coughlin nods.

"You threw it kind of easy," offers Claire.

"Why did I do that? Wouldn't it be faster to throw it hard?"

"No," maintains Claire. "Because Willy's not that far away from you and it would probably just bounce offa' him then, or go out of the circle and he would have to go get it and then it would really slow things down."

Aaron's hand is up. It's clear, even at six, that he is a versatile and talented athlete and loves any chance to throw a ball—or talk about it! "If you were throwing at Amy or somebody all the way across the circle, you'd have to throw harder, though."

"So you noticed," summarizes Mr. Coughlin, naming specific behaviors with key words that can be quick reminders later, "that I used careful aim and a just-hard-enough throw."

"I'm going to throw it again and this time I want you to watch Willy and notice what he does that makes the catching part fast and in-control." After the class has noted that Willy keeps his eyes on Mr. Coughlin and his hands ready in his lap, the game begins. The modeling took only a few minutes and the chance for application was offered right away, important timing for these six-year-olds.

Model social as well as physical behaviors.

Some modeling addresses social rather than physical controls. Mr. Roth is determined that his fourth grade classroom will be one in which it is fine to make a mistake. It is a message he conveys day-in and day-out in a number of ways, from the poster on the wall that says "The only person who doesn't make a mistake is a person who never does anything" to the stories culled from his own everyday life which often include an error in thinking and the learning he gained from it. It is not a message accepted easily by his nine-year-old students who are painfully aware and critical of their own and their peers' imperfections.

"When we do an activity like Number Equations, we will sometimes make mistakes. I want us to be able to notice mistakes in a way that is honest and respectful so that we can learn from them. Today is the 4th. Jocelyn (an able math student), please make up an equation for the 4th that has a mistake in it. I'm going to be a student who catches the mistake. Watch me and notice how I respond."

"One hundred divided by twenty is four," offers Jocelyn, writing it on the chart.

Mr. Roth looks thoughtful for a moment and then slowly puts his hand up. Hamming it up just a bit, he switches chairs, mimes calling upon himself, moves back to his student chair and says, "I think that one hundred divided by twenty is five."

"What did you notice?"

"You didn't shoot your hand up really fast, like: 'Ooh, ooh, I see a mistake!'" Kelly mimes an over-eager response.

"You kept your voice nice and didn't sound know-it-all."

"You didn't laugh or roll your eyes."

"You said what you thought was right, not that Jocelyn was wrong."

Mr. Roth reframes in positive terms. "So honest and respectful mistake-noticing means that we stop and think first, and use a polite voice and body language when we suggest someone made a mistake."

"Yeah, 'cause it could be you the next time!" blurts Hank. Smiles of recognition reply.

Mr. Roth is pleased that his students recognize the helpful and not-so-helpful details. He also knows that habits don't change easily and that eyes will roll and hands will wave excitedly at a mistake, perhaps not today with this lesson fresh in their minds, but tomorrow or surely next week. And he will remind, redirect, and reinforce—always respectfully, as he has asked them to do when they notice others' mistakes.

Choose activities that fit the group at this particular time.

Choosing activities highlights the teacher's role as balance-keeper and as knower-of-the-group. The season of the school year, the group's degree of cohesiveness and its temperament are all factors in determining which activities will be most beneficial.

Is it the beginning of the year, before the children even know each others' names? Naming, introduction, or interview games are good. Is this a group of serious scholars who could use some lightening up? Perhaps Zoom or, with older students, Ra-De-O, and when they are comfortable enough, I Love Ya Honey (But I Just

Can't Smile). Have the last three mornings of antics at Meeting and messy transitions let you know that this group needs tight structure and focus at every turn? Or maybe you have a group with a very low sense of academic self-esteem. Memorizing a serious and beautiful poem together will help them look at themselves differently.

There are many categories of activities with a number of modifications and variations that will help meet the day-to-day needs of every group:

- Physical/high energy activities
- Silly/fun activities
- Intellectual games/puzzle activities
- Creative/artistic activities

Use your observations and knowledge of your ever-growing group as you design a menu of different activities for and with your class. *Appendix E* offers a wide variety of Group Activities to help you get started.

Group Activity Responsibilities

In implementing and assessing Group Activity, keep the following general responsibilities in mind.

Teachers' responsibilities

- **Choose a variety of activities which are age-appropriate and include all skill levels**
- **Make sure many different kinds of activities are represented—physical, intellectual, artistic**
- **Give directions that are simple, clear, and consistent**
- **Make sure everyone knows the rules of activities**
- **Select activities that are non-competitive**
- **Model being playful or enthusiastic without being silly**
- **Stop the activity and regroup if it's not going well**

Students' responsibilities

- **Participate fully in all activities**
- **Interact with all classmates**
- **Show respect and support for the efforts of all participants**
- **Have fun without being silly**
- **Work hard without being competitive**
- **Follow the rules of activities**

FINE TUNINGS

I know that activities should be fun, but my class gets really silly and doesn't take them seriously. Any suggestions?

You are right to draw a distinction between silliness and playfulness. While play can enhance learning, silliness is distracting and gets in the way of group engagement. Monitoring the tone is an important teacher job in Morning Meeting. Don't be afraid to stop an activity if it feels too silly or unfriendly and reminders and redirections have not helped

The next step is to do some observation or reflection. Is the silliness coming from a couple of students or is it widespread? If it comes from one or two students, consider whether there is something about the particular activity that makes it hard for them to join wholeheartedly. You may need to speak to them individually to say what you notice, and ask them to think of ways they can help Group Activity work better.

If the troubling attitude is group-wide, it's time to look at the activities themselves. Perhaps it's time for very structured activities that offer challenge, that help the group take itself more seriously. Remember that it is Group Activity, not Group Game.

If varying the type of activity doesn't help, sharing what you notice with your students and inviting their thoughts about what's happening may.

The same students seem to "star" in Group Activity. How can I address this?

We must make sure that the variety of activities we present call upon many different modalities. Though it is important that everyone be able to participate in all the activities, it is true that—except for a few extraordinarily well-rounded individuals—we all have different areas where we shine and areas where we struggle. Group Activities allow us to see ourselves and each other, teachers included, in those shinings and those struggles.

Some of us are graceful and coordinated; some are verbally quick and playful. Some have terrific recall and excel at memory games and recitation; others are theatrical and can pantomime any emotion down to its every nuance. Still others have a gift of melody that enables a class to sound beautiful when they sing together.

Making sure our activities engage many different aptitudes ensures that all children will have experience in the role of leader and in the role of "leaner." All will get to feel foolish and all will get to feel smart. Robby learns that when he stands next to Casey he can, in fact, carry a tune. Meg learns that if she forgets a line in the skit, she can glance at Noah who will remember and give her a cue.

As the group comes to know and rely upon each other, a group intelligence develops that enables some brilliant moments of ensemble play, times when the class pulls off something together which is clearly more than the sum of their individual efforts.

Corporations pay big dollars these days to experts who present seminars and teach employees the skills of team-playing and attempt to build group intelligence. It is the way workers must learn to work, say futurists. Schoolchildren engaged in a Group Activity practice it every day.

There is a boy in my class who hangs back and never partici-pates in Group Activity. How can I encourage him to join?

This is a situation in which a teacher's knowledge of her individual students is crucial. What does this boy choose to do at recess or choice times? What are his areas of comfort and skill? If it is Gerry, who excels at anything with the suffix "-ball," I would choose something involving ball-throwing. If it is Casey, who has a wealth of information about the latest world conflict or most recent movie blockbuster, then I would structure an activity around cur-rent events. If the activity is a new one for your group, you might elicit this student's help ahead of time to try it out and co-teach it to the group with you.

I've run out of ideas for Group Activities and it's starting to feel like one more thing I have to make "fun." I'm feeling burdened by it and my students don't seem to be having much fun with it either. Am I just not creative enough?

It's true that in Group Activity, as in almost everything in our class-rooms, the teacher's sense of engagement and pleasure is conta-gious. And the reverse is true. If you are consistently feeling unin-spired and weighed down by a certain part of the routine, your class will perceive it.

Sometimes we work too hard to make things "fun." Play and engagement are as much about a way of doing something as they are about the content of what we are doing. Remind yourself that although the best learning is highly entertaining, it is not your role as a teacher to be an entertainer. Group Activities needn't be one more thing; they can spring from the program you are already working hard to plan for your students.

Picture these scenes. A group of seventh-graders, totally involved, mentally wrestle together with a tricky logic problem. Down the hall, the third-graders are clapping out the syllables in their weekly list of spelling words, feet tapping along. In the pri-mary room, the kindergarten and first grade class are proudly

Group Activities can spring from the daily curriculum; these children clap out the syllables in their weekly list of spelling words.

"reading" in unison a poem hand-lettered in large clear print on the easel in the circle. In another primary class, students are using their bodies to make a beaver lodge and act out the activities of a beaver colony, representing and extending the learning they have gained from their study of beavers who inhabit a nearby pond.

All of these activities come straight from curriculum in the room. They are not imported just for activity time and they are not games. They meet the criteria for Group Activity perfectly: they are noncompetitive and inclusive; they require attention and alertness; they build the group's sense of how they can problem-solve together; they develop a group voice, intelligence, and identity.

Finally, consider shifting some of the responsibility for making the activities work from you to your students. Many teachers, after introducing a new activity, ask the group two reflective questions:

    1.What made it work?

    2.What made it fun?

This gets the children thinking about how they work together and leads to an increase in their investment.

News
and
Announcements

The Group Activity finished, Ms. Adams turns to the chart on an easel next to her, physically adjusting it a bit so that it is visible to all in the circle. Her third-graders take this moment to adjust themselves, too, settling themselves for the News and Announcements in Morning Meeting. The message on the chart involves some questions about months of the year and days of the month, a current topic in the class's math program. (See chart on page 100.)

Ms. Adams points to the blanks provided for the date. "No one filled in the date yet. Who can tell me the date today?" Almost every hand goes up.

"Let's hear how some people figured out what day of the month it is."

"I looked at the calendar and I knew that today is the last Monday of the month. And I read what month it is at the top of the calendar page. But I remembered that anyway."

"I used tally marks from our calendar countdown on the chalk board."

Ms. Adams hands a fat green marker to a child whose hand is up. "Alyssa, fill in the date, please."

News and Announcements continues with a student selected to read the message, followed by a discussion about months of the year based on what students have filled in at the bottom of the chart. Together, students check the accuracy of their filled-in answers and complete the remaining one. Their teacher points out that months always begin with upper case letters and gives a mini-lesson on articulation when she notices that most of the class isn't saying the "th" sound at the end of the ordinal numbers on the chart.

Hello, Great Thinkers!

Today is _____ ___, ___.

Today _Sharla_ will lead our Greeting. _Charlie_ and _Tate_ will share. We will recite our October poem.

This month is ending. How many days are left? _5_ How many days have passed? _25_ What month follows October? _November_

What month is the _____th month of the year?

1st _January_
7th _October_
10th _October_
5th _May_

Have a super productive day.

Pointing to the last sentence on the chart, the teacher reads it again. "What do I mean by 'productive'? Let's think of some synonyms." Hands go up and ideas are ventured.

"Great"

"Terrific."

"Smart."

"Enjoyful."

Ms. Adams acknowledges each adjective with a nod, commenting after the last, "Yes, we do feel good when we're productive. We enjoy it. You are giving me great synonyms for a word like 'fantastic.' Can you think of a word or a couple of words that means almost the exact same thing as productive?"

There is a long pause before Tyler's hand goes up. "A working hard day."

"Yes, that defines it well!"

Ms. Adams glances at her watch. "I have just a couple of announcements about today. This morning those who didn't bake yesterday will be baking corn bread with Rafe's mother. Other than that we will have a regular Tuesday. You've paid attention through a long meeting. Now let's stand." They push their chairs back, anticipating what's to come. "Stretch up, get the kinks out, now hug yourselves tight, heads up, now down to your knees. Let's come up slowly . . ."

Purposes and Reflections

News and Announcements provides information and group academic work through a message written by the teacher on a chart each day. While the contents and format of the message change as children get older, as well as the way it is read before and during Meeting, the methods and purposes stay the same.

Before Meeting begins, children read the message as they enter the room and follow any instructions on it. The chart is then moved into the Meeting circle and used as the basis for the last component of Meeting each day. During that time, the message on the chart is read, then discussed with quick activities based on the chart.

Purposes of News and Announcements

- **Eases the transition into the classroom day and makes children feel excited about what they'll be learning**

- **Develops and reinforces language, math, and other skills in a meaningful and interactive way**

- **Builds community through shared written information**

You may want to browse through *Appendix F* to familiarize yourself with some samples of News and Announcements charts before continuing and use them for reference in the sections that follow.

News and Announcements eases the transition into the classroom day and makes children feel excited about what they'll be learning.

The chart invites children to participate even before Meeting begins.

Seeing an attractive and interesting chart waiting at the beginning of the day is one way of letting children know that their teacher is ready for them, has thought about the day, and is welcoming them to it. It supplements face-to-face greetings and "check-ins" rather than replacing them.

Information on the chart acclimates students to the day and allows them to reflect on learning and events of previous days. The chart often invites them to begin participating even before Meeting: "Draw a food that you saw on our trip to the store yesterday." "Can you find a spelling mistake or two in this message?" "List one fact you know about Sojourner Truth."

Included on the chart is a message from the teacher, telling the children about something they will be learning that day. The teacher may highlight one thing from all of the content that will be taught that day which will make the children feel excited about what's ahead. This message can also include notes about "specialists," announcements about anything happening which is out of the ordinary (visitors, assemblies, field trips, etc.), and what will happen directly after the close of Meeting. In this way, News and Announcements helps prepare children not only for the beginning of the school day and Meeting but also for the shift from Meeting to the rest of the classroom day.

News and Announcements develops and reinforces language, math and other skills in a meaningful and interactive way.

For younger children who are learning to read and write, the daily use of the written News and Announcements chart teaches reading, language arts, and math skills through meaningful information and relevant questions. The language patterns used on the chart are deliberately predictable and repetitious from day to day. They include familiar sight vocabulary and reflect content from classroom life which makes it interesting to the children.

"Freddy is first. Maura is the door holder. Today is . . ." These

*During Meeting, the teacher uses the chart to ask questions or play
quick games which offer challenges but allow success.*

simple sentence patterns, to which even the youngest quickly
become accustomed, teach letter and number recognition, phonic
skills, word families, and spelling and language patterns.

Including one or two sentences at the end of the chart that are
not predictable or repetitious lets children develop and practice
strategies for independent reading of unfamiliar language. The content of these sentences is drawn from the day's activities or curriculum. It helps motivate students, provides another opportunity
to orient them to the day, and presents vocabulary that they will
encounter again. "We will finger-paint." "We will talk about our
spider today."

During Morning Meeting, the teacher asks questions or plays
quick games based upon the information on the chart. For example:

- Who can find the letter "t"?

- Who can find two letters that go together and make the
  sound "ba"?

- Who can tell a number sentence for the number five?

- Who can name something in our room that we have five of?

Questions and activities can include a range of skills that offer challenges but allow success. Children need to start their day with feelings of mastery and competence. Teachers keep these questions and games fast-paced, especially when individual children are coming up to the chart to write or find something, so that the entire group is kept involved.

Before there are readers in the group, the teacher often stands at the chart in the morning, helping children read it before Morning Meeting, or the reading can be done at Morning Meeting. As children become able to read the chart on their own, teachers often pair those who are not yet readers with partners who have learned to be "reading guides." When children help each other in this way, both partners benefit and what is learned can extend far beyond the content of the chart, far beyond the acquisition of phonics skills. The following piece of writing, an excerpt from an essay my daughter wrote as part of an application to secondary school, is testimony to what is learned. In it she remembers her experience helping a classmate who had severe difficulty learning to decode words.

By fourth grade Pauline had begun waiting for me in the mornings next to the chart we were supposed to read as we came into the room. She would run her fingers over and over the words, her mouth moving slowly, trying to reach the word that would most make sense. I first began to help her by standing next to her and reading aloud the message. I was filled with empathy as I began to see what a struggle the simple things I did daily were for her. A few days later I asked if she wanted help with some of the more difficult words, and within weeks we had established an understanding that she would point to the words that she did not recognize and we would sound them out together. This continued to work, and as we grew more comfortable with each other she asked me if I would help her read the message aloud, sounding out the words. From there on I can remember every morning

*standing by the chart and working endlessly on the same "Good morning"
or "Today we will be . . ." I have no memory of learning to read myself, but
I do clearly remember the hours I spent helping Pauline.*

For older children, who have moved from learning to read and
write to reading and writing to learn, the message will be more
complex. Often teachers find that the format of a "letter to the
class" works well. "Dear Friendly Workers," it might begin one day.
On the Friday of a week of rain, "Dear Soggy Students" might be
the salutation. The date is still included. Often the message
includes an item that lets students learn about each other — "Who
has a birthday this month?" "Who has the middle name 'Rose'?" or
a tally like, "Sign your name here if you have a cat."

Reminders of responsibilities—"Jamie leads Sharing today"—
may be listed along with news or reminders about the day: "We
will have a visitor from _____" or "Bring your writing to
Meeting today and be ready to share your opening sentence."
Punctuation errors may be deliberately inserted for students to
find and fix or math problems presented for solutions.

*The chart message on this April morning invites
kindergartners to "draw something that grows."*

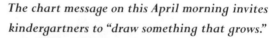

*A seventh grader points out a spelling error in the morning
message, an error deliberately inserted by the teacher.*

Even with older students, however, this is not a time for new
instruction. It is a time for practicing skills and for peer learning.
It is a lively, short warm-up with the goal of sending students into
the day feeling engaged and capable.

News and Announcements builds community through shared written information.

Responsible citizens stay informed about what's going on in their
community. News and Announcements is one way that we can
allow students to practice that responsibility in their classrooms.

When I read my local newspaper each morning, I skim for names
I know, news that affects my town, meetings I might want to attend,
births, deaths, land transfers, or environmental issues I care about. I
follow a similar process with the *New York Times* for national and inter-
national news. I must spot something in the headlines which piques
my interest or makes me realize that this news is of import to me.
Sometimes what catches my attention is not purely informational
but engages my skills at vocabulary or logic (the puzzle pages) or

simply makes me smile (comics). I pick and choose and assemble a collage of news and announcements that keeps me informed about the community of which I define myself as a citizen.

The daily message we create for our students shares much with my daily newspaper perusing. However, we do the picking and choosing of items and assemble them for our students, using what we know about their development, their skills, their pleasures, and the programs of our classrooms. We must make the content full of pertinent information, with inviting activities—and we must expect that all will use it.

Highlights of News and Announcements

- **Features a written message which welcomes and greets students as they enter the room**
- **Gets children excited about what they'll be learning that day**
- **Adds predictability and structure to entering the classroom**
- **Contributes to students' sense of safety and being cared for by letting them know that the teacher has prepared for the day and is ready for them**
- **Affords a fun and interactive way to teach written language, math, and other skills**
- **Conveys that reading is a valuable way to get information you need**
- **Builds community through shared written information**
- **Provides a "warm-up" for the day's activities**
- **Eases the transition from Morning Meeting to the rest of the day**

You may want to review the samples of News and Announcements charts in *Appendix F* and the ideas for creating them in *Appendix G* before going on.

GETTING STARTED

Introduce News and Announcements.

Let students know that every day there will be a message from you with news about the day which they should read before Meeting and that it will be used at the end of Meeting as well. Model reading and reacting to the message for that day. Depending upon the age and reading level of your students, you may read to them, have them read in chorus, take turns reading, have one student read while others follow along, or have older children paraphrase what's on the chart.

Plan the logistics of the message chart.

Most teachers prefer using a chart stand and easel paper for their message, rather than the chalkboard. In most rooms, this makes it easier to physically move and incorporate into the Meeting circle. Using paper and markers eliminates the risks of smudges and erasures and allows the chart to be saved and posted after Meeting time. Some teachers put old charts in the class library for children to read during Language Arts or send them home with individual children, such as the Student of the Day or the Line Leader.

You will need to choose a spot for the chart that is prominent and greets students as they enter the room. It should be a spot that will not interrupt early morning traffic flow, however, when several children are clustered around it, reading or responding to the message. Keeping it in the same spot every morning helps make it part of the classroom routine.

Tailor content, format, and activities to your particular class.

Part of what makes a morning message chart of real interest is its pertinence to the classroom life of this particular group at this particular time. To be real and immediate, our messages must be specific to each day and class. Although it is fine, even essential, to develop a boilerplate, if the sentences don't change, then the message isn't "News." If they are irrelevant to the day, they aren't "Announcements."

With younger groups in which most students are not yet fluent readers, even the predictable parts of the chart are specific to the day, including such information as today's date, the name of today's line leader, today's door holder. Additional content usually springs from current activities: "We will work with clay today" or "Look at our egg before Meeting."

With older groups, where reading skills are established, there is room for more variation in format, but the information should still derive from classroom activities and interests. Perhaps it's World Series time and excitement is high; the chart might feature a math problem involving statistics from yesterday's game. Recess didn't work well yesterday? The chart might direct students to be prepared to share at Morning Meeting one way they think they can make it better today. If capitalization is something you note many students struggling with in their writing, the News and Announcements activity could involve discussion of which words should be capitalized.

Using this type of content, the message becomes one more way to communicate with students about ongoing classroom affairs and subjects; it should not require separate and additional content creation.

Keep it simple.

Particularly in older grades, it can be tempting to make the chart comprehensive, squeezing in just one more thing students really ought to be thinking about, one more type of spelling mistake. This can get overwhelming, both for the students who must read and act upon the chart information and for the teacher who must create it.

Remember—the purposes of the News and Announcements component are to welcome and greet students, to orient them and get them excited about their day, sometimes to accomplish an administrative task which doesn't require elaboration, and to use the written format of the chart for a quick "warm-up" skill-builder. Resist the temptation to launch into a full-blown lesson based on a spelling error students didn't catch or to list everything students will need to know about tomorrow's field trip on the chart.

Instead, file away the spelling error for a mini-lesson before writing time later this week. Perhaps next week a message chart will feature six examples of words with that spelling pattern to be discovered. And if the field trip requires substantial preparation and reminders, then a separate field trip meeting in the afternoon is in order.

News and Announcements, coming at the end of Morning Meeting, serves as a transition into the rest of the day. We want students to leave the Meeting feeling a sense of their competence and equipped to navigate their day. It is important, therefore, that the last few minutes of Meeting be well-paced and uncluttered, not crammed with hurried instructions and partially-understood communications, no matter how well-intentioned.

Also resist the temptation to post your schedule for the day on the chart. While this information is important and the schedule should be posted somewhere, the chart is not the place for it. If the chart simply contains a list of the day's activities, many children will stop reading it. Instead, the content of the chart should change daily, highlighting perhaps one thing from all the content you'll be teaching that day.

News and Announcements Responsibilities

In implementing and assessing News and Announcements, keep the following general responsibilities in mind.

Teachers' responsibilities

- **Prepare the message chart before students arrive**
- **Model good printing or cursive writing and correct usage in the written message**
- **Use predictable language patterns**
- **Incorporate ongoing curriculum into the message and the activity**

- Select the best format for reading the chart in Meeting (unison, teacher reading with students, one reader, several readers, paraphrasing)

- Choose individual students to unscramble, decode, find errors, etc. while still keeping the whole group involved

- Vary the kinds of skills featured in the chart activity

- End with announcements to help students make a transition to the rest of the day

Students' responsibilities

- Read the message upon entering the room

- Follow any directions in the message

- Read or follow along with the reading of the chart during Meeting

- Participate in activities based upon the chart before or during Meeting

- Listen to announcements presented

FINE TUNINGS

My students really like reading the message chart, but I find it hard to keep thinking of new things to write each day. I feel like it's taking me more time than it should to prepare the chart.

You have lots of company, particularly among teachers of students in intermediate and upper grades, where the predictable sentence starters and additional sentence or two that are just right for primary students are not enough.

Remember the caution from "Getting Started" about using the daily life of the classroom as a springboard for your message and activity. Look to your ongoing curriculum and to your general observations and knowledge of your class as sources rather than trying to think of fascinating, additional tidbits. Do your students adore riddles? Are codes really fun for them right now? Are they all really excited about the upcoming Olympics?

Some teachers have found that having a different but predictable topic for each day of the week helps them vary the content of their charts while removing the stress of total invention. Monday's chart might always feature a question or tally about weekend activities while Tuesday's chart might pose a math problem, for example. The suggestions for special topics and elements for charts in *Appendix G* illustrate many possibilities teachers have used as successful starters which they then customize for their Morning Meetings.

What's the difference between Group Activity and the News and Announcements activity?

Their basic purposes differ. A primary goal of Group Activity is building a sense of whole-group spirit, whereas the purpose of a News and Announcements activity is to stimulate children's academic motivation and give them a chance to practice skills.

Based as they are upon the chart, News and Announcements activities nearly always center upon written communication. The learning interaction often involves one student or a small, spontaneous group of students working with the material before the Meeting convenes.

There is, of course, overlap. News and Announcements activities can and often do build a group's sense of itself; Group Activities can and often do center upon language arts or math skills. This is one of those areas requiring some attention to overall balance. If the day's Group Activity involves math equations, you will probably want to plan a different sort of focus for the chart activity.

I have a class with twenty-seven sixth graders and I find that there is often not enough time for doing News and Announcements with an activity, particularly if our Group Activity has really "grabbed" the students. I can't keep students longer than thirty minutes because we team with other teachers and students for the rest of the morning's subjects.

It's fine to vary the Morning Meeting format, based upon your judgments about your class and what works for them. I remember a class of seventh- and eighth-graders I observed where a boy's sharing about a favorite old teddy bear prompted a spontaneous sort of Group Activity—all the members of the circle shared ways they helped themselves get to sleep at night. All the posturing which can be so prevalent at that age dropped away as, one after another, stories of beloved stuffed friends, remnants of fuzzy baby blankets, rhythmic head rocking or foot circling emerged. When the stories were completed, only a few minutes of Meeting time remained—just enough for their teacher to make an announcement or two about the day ahead. It would have been a shame to curtail this sharing in order to fit in work with a chart or a different activity.

Some decisions about time variations happen on the spot, as in the example above. Other times, teachers know ahead of time and plan to shorten or omit certain components. Perhaps a new activity is going to be taught, or perhaps Sharing involves models of solar powered appliances that students have been building in science. A fine sense of pacing allows time for a group to fully engage while not letting things drag. Teachers should keep in mind the purposes and range of activities for each component of Morning Meeting and make sure that all are encompassed over time, not necessarily in each Meeting.

A
Silent
Bulldozer of
School Reform

Morning Meeting is a silent bulldozer in the field of school reform," proclaimed Maurice Sykes several years ago when he was deputy superintendent of the Washington, D.C. public schools. I was happily predisposed to respect and accept his observations since I had often found him to be a master at crafting just the right phrase to describe essential notions as well as an astute observer of elementary classrooms.

This time, however, his metaphor just didn't sit well. A bull-dozer? I closed my eyes and let the images of bulldozers I had known flow by. Dust . . . blistering yellow . . . noise . . . clanging . . . beep . . . beep . . . rubble. But wait, erase the clanging and beeping. Maurice had a different bulldozer in mind—a silent one. I tried to imagine it—this bright and powerful machine scooping and clearing and smoothing its way silently across the landscape.

The landscape in my imagination was a construction site, I real-ized. Construction. Hmmm. The word and its variants tumbled around in my head—construct, constructive, constructivist. I extended the metaphor as I began to think about the role of a bull-dozer differently. Yes, it makes piles of rubble, but as a preface to clearing them away. It follows the wrecking ball and prepares the earth for new creation. New structures cannot be erected where old ones are still standing or where piles of debris litter the ground. Building requires a bulldozer.

I brought my interpretation to a group of colleagues who had come together for a discussion on Morning Meeting. What does Morning Meeting clear away, I wondered. And what is to be constructed in that clearing?

There were several moments of silence and then, around the circle, the responses came—eloquent and thoughtful every one.

"Morning Meeting clears time. The beginning of the school day is so often a jumble, kids doing seat work while teachers take attendance, do lunch counts. Morning Meeting makes time for teachers and children to be focused with each other on important things."

"And space. It clears a space for those things to happen. Making that space carries over, and it transforms the entire environment of the classroom."

"Morning Meeting clears away an old way of seeing children in a classroom to make way for a new approach. The new approach has children at its center and views community as a powerful instrument in teaching and learning."

"Morning Meeting clears away the barriers of social status and other inequities. Everyone's on the floor, on the same level, in a circle, looking at each other. Each morning it levels the ground, clears away yesterday's stuff and we start fresh. There are lots of opportunities for growth in the aftermath of a bulldozer's work."

"Yes, a bulldozer clears a space. And in that space can remain a hole, or an empty skyscraper full of unrentable space, or a sturdy, useful building. And it's work, filling in that space. We're always constructing. But Morning Meeting gives us the tools."

"Those tools, the simple strategies and clear structures, move us in the direction of profound goals. Sometimes we don't even know the full import of what's happening for a long time. That's the silent part."

It was a defining conversation. I looked around and summed up the years of teaching experience that the seven of us brought to the table. 135, I estimated. We wondered together, listened to each other, and built upon each others' ideas until a full new understanding emerged. Exploring my query in a social context had deepened and enriched both the process and its result immeasurably. It was, I realized with a jolt, just what Morning Meeting helps children to do.

Our meeting even mirrored the components of Morning Meeting, though without titles and overt structures. We had drifted in casually, saying our hellos to colleagues, smiles and nods of acknowledgment flowing back and forth and around the circle at our table. Greeting drifted into Sharing complete with questions and comments. I just can't get rid of this cough. How did the workshop in New Orleans go? The closing on your house is held up again? You must be so frustrated! And then on to our Group Activity—a planned and purposeful dialogue about Morning Meeting. And before we adjourned, some announcements—We'll reconvene at two o'clock. Remember to bring your calendars.

Some of us headed to our classrooms, some to another meeting, some back to our offices. Though the tasks that awaited each of us were different, we left invigorated and reminded of our common mission, our fascination with the process of learning, and our passion for good schooling for all.

I remembered an observation by educator Suzanne Goldsmith that I had recently read in *Teaching Tolerance*. "Communities are not built of friends, or of groups of people with similar styles and tastes, or even of people who like and understand each other. They are built of people who feel they are a part of something that is bigger than themselves." (Goldsmith 1998, 4) Morning Meeting builds that kind of community.

Appendix A

What Children Are Learning in
Each Component of Morning Meeting

Excerpted from *Morning Meeting Handbook*

Compiled by Washington, D.C. public school teachers
enrolled in Responsive Classroom courses 1992–1993

Greeting

*When children are **greeting** each other, they are learning to:*

- Acknowledge the presence of themselves and others
- Recognize first and last names
- Be courteous, considerate, and caring
- Become more secure in a formal social situation
- Follow directions
- Develop auditory perception
- Acknowledge different cultures
- Gain a sense of community and belonging
- Articulate thoughts concisely
- Gain self-esteem
- Imitate words and motions
- Communicate orally in front of a group
- Communicate clearly in a loud voice
- Remember games and words
- Make eye contact with their audience
- Follow left to right progression

- Sit and stand with good posture
- Wait their turn
- Pay attention and focus on the speaker
- Welcome classmates to the group
- Help classmates feel valued, liked, and wanted
- Express their feelings respectfully
- Locate the position of the greeter and position themselves in order to be greeted when they come in late
- Speak in complete sentences
- Practice self-control
- Understand spoken information
- Recall the sequence of sounds
- Use new vocabulary
- Recall details
- Use appropriate body language
- Develop new and different ways to greet each other
- Speak at the appropriate time
- Show respect for themselves and others
- Enhance language skills
- Develop sequencing skills

Sharing

*When children are **sharing**, they are learning to:*

- Develop communication skills in expressive and receptive language
- Develop leadership skills
- Retell experiences in sequence
- Use critical thinking skills

- Organize ideas
- Identify the main idea
- Accept the values of others
- Respect the opinions, experiences, and cultures of others
- Become comfortable as the center of attention
- Select appropriate thoughts to share
- Ask respectful questions and give meaningful comments
- Express opinions
- Draw conclusions
- Make comparisons
- Distinguish between reality and fantasy
- Infer causes
- Take turns
- Gain knowledge through others' experiences
- Pay compliments
- Build self-esteem
- Respect others' property
- Become more familiar with themselves and others
- Develop empathy and compassion
- Enhance language arts skills, including listening and public speaking

Group Activity

*When students are participating in **Group Activity**, they are learning to:*

- Work together for a common good
- Solve problems
- Think quickly and creatively

- Identify patterns and sequences
- Identify action words and directions
- Improve their gross motor skills
- Play and follow simple rules
- Empathize
- Increase muscle control, hand-eye coordination, and balance
- Increase self-confidence
- Use creative language
- Participate in a variety of games and activities
- Interact easily with classmates
- Choose new as well as familiar activities
- Repeat a message to others
- Participate actively in the group life of the class
- Make up word games
- Participate in cooperative learning
- Learn through movement
- See the fun in learning and have a good time
- Feel a part of the group
- Support each other

News and Announcements

When children are participating in **News and Announcements,** *they are learning to:*

- Participate in group oral reading
- Recognize letter sounds
- Recognize upper and lower case letters
- Recognize the names of classmates

- Follow directions and work independently
- Count, add, subtract, multiply, and divide
- Recall familiar words
- Identify rhyming words
- Identify and construct letters of the alphabet
- Write their own names
- Follow left and right progressions
- Identify verbs, adjectives, compound words, and pronouns
- Distinguish opposites
- Identify and use various punctuation marks
- Take responsibility for reading and spelling
- Distinguish picture clues and context
- Use letter names to represent sounds
- Build number concepts and problem-solving skills
- Strengthen predicting, sequencing, estimation, and probability skills
- Determine predictable chart patterns, configuration, sentence structure, and letter formation
- Use grammar properly
- Use information including seasons, months of the year, and days of the week
- Develop skills in reading, language arts and math
- Organize and plan
- Understand transitions and orientations

Appendix B

Letter to Parents about

Morning Meeting

Here is a letter we have developed to provide information to parents about Morning Meeting. We strongly encourage you to use it as a "boilerplate" and to adapt and edit it to meet your needs.

Dear Parents,

There's a wonderful new beginning to your child's school day! It's called Morning Meeting. Each morning, first thing, the teacher gathers the class together. Desks are quietly moved aside and children form a circle with their chairs or sit on the floor on a rug or on carpet squares. In a circle, everyone can see and hear each other.

To start Morning Meeting, children greet each other by name. Sometimes the "Good Morning" is passed right around the circle. Sometimes children get up and greet each other across the circle with a handshake and a "Good Morning!" Every morning, your child starts the day by hearing his or her name called by a classmate in a friendly and cheerful manner.

Next, children have the chance to share some news of interest with the class. Usually three or four children will share each day. Sharing might be about a visit to a grandparent, or about a visit to a library or a store. It might be sharing a special rock from a rock collection, or a special happening with a friend or sibling. It might be sharing school work of which the student is especially proud. After the student shares, s/he asks the circle, "Are there any questions or comments?" In the conversation that follows, children learn much about each other, especially respect for someone else's ideas!

After Sharing, there is an activity for the whole class. Some days it might be singing or learning a poem. Other days it might be a math or language game. The activity time helps the class feel their strength as a whole group. They find out they can cooperate and solve problems. They can have fun and learn a lot together.

The last part of Morning Meeting is called News and Announcements. During this time, students think about the day ahead. The teacher may challenge them with interesting written messages on the News and Announcements Chart. The teacher may take this time to teach a reading, spelling, or punctuation skill. S/he may ask students to read the chart together. The message is like an advertisement for some upcoming event in the school day.

Morning Meeting lasts about 20 minutes. In Headstart and PreK, it is shorter. In grades 2–3, it may be 20–30 minutes and in grades 4–6, it is never longer than 30 minutes.

Teachers and principals say Morning Meeting is great for learning cooperation, self-worth, responsibility for a job, and a sense of community. When children greet each other, they learn courtesy, how to respond politely when someone speaks to them, how to care for their classmates. When children are greeted they hear their name and feel proud and important. Likewise, when children share, they feel that their ideas are valued and that their classmates are interested in them. They learn how to ask good questions and to make respectful comments. They learn how to be good listeners.

In Morning Meeting children learn to value themselves and their class. They increase their self-confidence and respect for others. They learn how to make good use of information. They learn how to solve problems and heal hurt feelings. Morning Meeting lets children know every day that school is a safe place where everyone's feelings and ideas are important.

To learn more about Morning Meeting, arrange to visit your child's class one day. You'll see for yourself why everyone is so excited about this start to the school day.

Appendix C

Modeling: A Teaching Technique

Throughout this book, the technique of modeling is referred to as a teaching strategy. Generally, teachers use modeling when they want to teach a very specific behavior and want children to imitate the demonstrated way of behaving. It is frequently used to introduce children to expected behaviors during Morning Meeting: how to move chairs safely and efficiently; how to do a formal handshake; how to be a good listener, etc. Below is a step-by-step example of how a teacher might use this technique to teach children to pass a friendly handshake around the circle.

Step 1: Teacher names and presents the desired behavior.

Example: "I want us to pass a friendly handshake. Watch what I do."

Step 2: The desired behavior is demonstrated by the teacher.

Example: Teacher reaches over and shakes the hand of a student next to her.

Step 3: Teacher asks students to notice and name the elements of the behavior. Teacher elicits the specific actions and expressions that made this a "friendly handshake."

Example: "What did you notice that made this a "friendly handshake?"
"You looked at Sean."
"You smiled."
"You turned your body so it was facing Sean."
"You took his hand."
"You said his name."
"What else did you notice about my handshake?"
"You shook his hand but not so hard."

Step 4: The teacher focuses on "tricky" parts.

Example: The teacher might now focus more attention on the hand-shake itself since it's critical in this greeting that the physical contact be safe and positive. The teacher would repeat steps 1–4 focusing on the handshake. "I want to be sure I give Sean a 'firm and gentle' handshake. Watch me."

"What made it 'firm'?"

"What made it 'gentle'?"

Step 5: Students practice "tricky" parts by demonstrating and noticing what works.

Example: The teacher asks for students to demonstrate: "Who thinks they can give a 'firm and gentle' handshake?" The teacher then asks the children watching questions like, "What did you notice about the handshake Emily gave Becky?"

Step 6: Students practice behaviors as a whole class.

Example: Teacher says, "Let's greet each other by sending a friendly handshake around the circle."

Step 7: Reinforce observed positive behaviors. This occurs both immediately following the modeling and at other points when desired behaviors are seen.

Example: "I saw people really look at each other. I heard names. I saw firm and gentle handshakes."

Step 8: Teacher continues to reinforce, remind, and redirect as needed. In addition to modeling desired behaviors, the teacher may at times want to playfully model "undesired" behaviors.

Example: The teacher takes hold of a student's hand by two fingers and asks, "Is this a firm handshake? Why not? Show me, what should I do to make this a firm handshake?"

Appendix D

Morning Meeting Greetings

As you try some of these Greetings in your classroom, remember the impor-
tance of keeping variety in the Greetings you use during Morning Meeting.
As children become familiar with the routines and rituals of Greeting, they
will start to make adaptations to old favorites and bring in new ideas of
their own. Keep a chart posted with your repertoire so that you and the
children can keep your daily Greetings fresh and fun!
To help you locate specific Greetings, they are sorted into the
following categories:

Beginning-of-the-School-Year Greetings

These are Greetings which are easy to teach and to do. Included
are Greetings which help children learn each others' names and
interests.

"Good Morning _____"

Some options:

- simple face to face
- with handshake
- with "high five"
- with pinky shake
- with a touch on the shoulder
- with a wave

Different Languages for "Good Morning"

Some options:

- Bonjour (French)
- Bonjourno (Italian)
- Shalom (Hebrew)
- Buenos Dias (Spanish)
- Ohieyo (Japanese)
- Gutten Morgan (German)
- Jen Dobre (Polish)
- Jambo (Swahili)
- Kale Mera (Greek)
- Sign language

A Formal Greeting

Students greet other students using last names: "Good Morning, Ms. Cather," "Good Morning, Mr. Loman." Students sometimes find this fun because they feel important being called by their last name.

Name Card Greeting

Place name cards in the center of the circle. A student chooses the top card from the pile and greets that person.

Introductions, Interests, and Favorites

Each child interviews a partner to prepare for this greeting.
This is my friend _____
and her/his favorite activity to do is _____.
(and her favorite book is _____).
(and his favorite food is _____).
(and he/she is good at _____) etc.

Pantomime Greeting

Each child pantomimes something about themselves (favorite activity, favorite food, favorite sport); others then greet and mimic the pantomime. The greetings are done by the whole class to each child.

Number Greeting

Place a slip of paper in a basket with a number on it for each person in the class. If there are 24 people in the class, put the numbers one through twelve in the basket with each number appearing twice. The meeting leader walks around with the basket and each person draws a number. The two people with number one come to the center of the circle to greet each other and so on until everyone has been greeted.

Skip Greeting

Each child skips a designated amount of spaces and greets the person who sits that many spaces away from him/her. The child who greeted someone then sits in the place of the child who was greeted. The children greet and switch places until everyone has been greeted. Let the students figure out a good number according to the amount of students in the class that day.

Cross-Circle Greetings

Children greet someone sitting across the circle from them. There can be many variations on this, such as cross-circle boy/girl greeting, cross-circle someone-you-haven't-spoken-to-yet-this-morning greeting, etc.

Butterfly Greetings

There are two versions of this simple greeting:
- Sit down butterfly: Two children sitting next to one another hook their thumbs together and wave their fingers in the sign

language sign for butterfly while saying good morning. This greeting then goes around the circle.

- Stand up butterfly: This is the same basic greeting except that students stand up and walk to greet someone across the circle.

Later-in-the-Year Greetings

These are Greetings which tend to take more instruction and practice in order to do well. They work best a few months into the school year, once a sense of community and trust has been established.

Hug Greeting

Children gently hug the child they are greeting. Practice making eye contact before hugging and hugging gently.

Spider Web Greeting

One child starts by holding a ball of yarn in one hand and one end of the yarn in the other. The child greets someone across the circle and gently rolls the ball of yarn across to the person while firmly holding on to the end of the string. The person who receives the ball of yarn holds a piece of the yarn down with one hand while greeting another child across the circle and rolling the ball of yarn to this child. This continues until everyone has been greeted and the yarn has created a web across the Meeting circle. To unravel the web, children greet each other in reverse order until the ball of yarn is wound up again.

Alphabetical Greeting

A simple "good morning" greeting with one big exception. Students must greet each other in alphabetical order. This is great for children learning how to alphabetize. However, even with older children, it can take quite a while to complete.

Book Character Greeting

During Book Week, students wear name tags of their favorite character. Greetings that week can be done using character names. At the end of the week, have students remove their name tags and see if they can remember each others' character names.

Compliment Greeting

Each child greets another child and gives a compliment. Be sure to model and set the expectation for compliments that reflect what children do, not what they wear or how they look.

Silent Greeting

Greetings are done silently with a part of your face (greet with your eyebrows, your eyes, your mouth, etc.) or a part of your body (your arms, shoulders, legs, etc.).

Elbow Rock

Created by a group of fifth-graders, this is a variation of the simple handshake greeting. Around the circle goes this greeting with each student saying good morning to the next, but instead of shaking hands, the students lock elbows and shake arms as they say their classmate's name. This can be trickier than it sounds as students will often have difficulty deciding which elbow to offer and which elbow of their partners to aim for.

The Quickie Righty/Lefty

When pressed for time, this "quickie" greeting can come in handy. One student begins by saying, "Good morning, everyone." The class responds in chorus, "Good morning." Each child turns to the right and greets that person and then to the left and greets that person. The one important rule to ensure that everyone feels greeted and acknowledged is that you have to make eye contact with the person you are greeting.

Physically Active Greetings

Ball Toss Greeting

Each child greets another child, then gently throws, rolls or bounces a ball to that child who in turn greets back (but keeps the ball to toss to another child). The greeting ends when the ball returns to the starter (each child is greeted once). If you're using a soft, small ball, throwing underhand works best. With a large, bouncy ball, rolling or bouncing the ball works best.

Ball Toss Variations for Middle and Upper Grades

Here are some variations which make the Ball Toss Greeting more challenging and serve to build cooperation for older children.

- Pass the greeting ball around the circle as explained above. Now the ball goes around one more time silently (with no greeting or talking) repeating the pattern it just made. Children will enjoy doing it several times this way and competing against the clock.

- Begin the first ball going around silently and at even intervals, add one or two more balls so that there are several balls going around in the pattern in which children greeted one another. Challenge the children to see if they can do it three times, without dropping and know exactly where to stop. You can also add the element of competition against the clock.

- Once the greeting ball has gone around the first time, have the children "undo the greeting pattern" by sending the ball back to the person who greeted them. This can be done with a greeting attached or silently. When the children get very good at remembering who greeted them, try ending your Morning Meeting with a ball toss in the reverse greeting pattern as they wish each other, "Have a good working day!" or whatever encouraging words the children decide they want to say that day.

Song and Chant Greetings for Younger Children

Hello

Hello, hello, hello and how are you?

I'm fine, I'm fine and I hope that you are too.

Repeat as many times as you want or need to in order to have everyone shake hands.

Rig-a-jig-jig

Half of the class makes an inner circle and the other half makes an outer circle. The inner circle moves around while the outer circle stays still or moves in the opposite direction. Everyone sings the following song. When the verse ends, the people in the inner circle greet the people in the outer circle. This continues for several rounds.

A rig-a-jig-jig and away we go,

Hi ho, hi ho, hi ho.

As I was walking down the street,

down the street, down the street,

A friend of mine I chanced to meet,

Hi ho, hi ho, hi ho.

Hello, Neighbor

Hello, neighbor, what d'ya say?

It's gonna be a wonderful day.

Clap your hands and boogie on down.

Give me a bump and turn around.

This is sung with the children standing up in a circle so they can "boogie on down" and give their neighbor a gentle hip bump. Designate partners at the beginning so everyone knows which neighbor to turn to.

Where Is _____ ?

To the tune of Frere Jacque
Group sings: Where is _____? Where is _____?
Child sings: Here I am, here I am.
Group sings: How are you today sir/ma'am?
Child sings: Very well, I thank you.
Group sings: We're glad you're here, we're glad you're here.

_____ is here

To the tune of Farmer in the Dell
All the children sing:
(Fill in the child's name) is here. _____ is here.
It's a great day because _____ is here.
All the children are seated in their circle. Tammy, who starts the greeting, stands up. She offers a handshake to Jeremy who is sitting next to her. Jeremy stands up to receive the handshake. At the same time that Tammy offers her handshake to Jeremy, the rest of the class starts to sing the song using Jeremy's name (Jeremy is here. Jeremy is here. . .). During the singing of the second line (It's a great day . . .), everyone claps their hands in rhythm to the tune. Tammy and Jeremy remain standing up while Jeremy then offers a handshake to the next child. It continues on until everyone is standing and the song comes back to Tammy, who is the last individual greeted. The greeting closes with everyone clapping and singing. "We all are here. We all are here. It's a great day because we all are here!"

Hickety-Pickety Bumble Bee

Hickety–Pickety Bumble Bee.
Won't you say your name for me.
_____ *(Child being greeted says his/her name or a child says the name of another.)*

Let's all say it.

Let's clap it.

Let's whisper it.

Let's turn off our voices and clap it.

Good Morning, Friends

Good morning, friends.

Two words so nice to say.

So clap your hands.

And stamp your feet.

And let's start together this way.

My name is _____

Each child takes a turn greeting the child next to him by saying:

My name is _____ and

I'm here to say,

I hope you have a very nice day.

Now the rest of the group joins in to say:

Ooh Ooh, Ooh Ooh Ooh *(first 2 are held long, last 3 are said quickly)*

You love me and I love you.

Shake shake, shake shake shake *(first 2 are held long, last 3 are said quickly)*

1, 2 you know what to do.

(The two children greeting shake hands.)

Chugga Chugga

Hey there _____ *(child being greeted is named).*

You're a real cool cat.

You've got a little of this *(snap fingers).*

And a little of that *(snap).*

So don't be afraid.

To boogie and jam.

Just stand up and chugga.

Fast as you can.

Chugga up, chugga chugga chugga chuggá. *(accent last syllable)*

Chugga down, chugga chugga chugga chuggá.

To the left, chugga chugga chugga chuggá.

To the right, chugga chugga chugga chuggá.

Song and Chant Greetings for Older Children

On the List

On the list, on the list.

Who's the next person on the list?

Since _____'s the next person on the list.

She'll/He'll tell you a story, now dig this!

(Child who is being greeted stands up and does a movement—wave, bow, dance step, etc.)

When you're up, you're up.

When you're down, you're down.

If you don't greet _____, you're up-side-down!

Side down . . . side down!

1, 2, 3, 4

1, 2, 3, 4, Come on _____ hit the floor.

(When name is called, child comes into the circle and does whatever he/she wants as a movement-bow, curtsy, wave, dance, wiggle, etc.)

We're so glad you're here today.

Hurray Hurray Hurray!

(Child moves back to circle at this point and attention moves to next child in circle.)

Roll Call

Group: Roll call, check the beat, check, check, check the beat.
Roll call, check the beat, check, check, check a-begin.
Child says: "My name is _____."
Group response: "Check!"
Child says: "They call me *(nickname)*."
Group response: "Check!"
Child says: "I am a student. That's what I am."*
Group response: "That's what s/he is."

* *Child chooses what to fill in here. Other examples might be "I am a baseball player"; "I am a poet"; "I am a friend."*

On the Phone

Group: Hey there *(child's name)*.
Child: Someone's calling my name.
Group: Hey there _____.
Child: Must be playing a game.
Group: Hey there _____you're wanted on the phone.
Child: Since it's my friend *(greeter names another child in circle)* , tell her/him I'm at home.
Whole Group: Just sitting on the sofa watching the clock.
                 Go tick tock, tick tock de wawa.
                 Tick tock, tick tock de wawa wa!

Hidey Hidey Hidey Ho

Call (one child): Hidey Hidey Hidey Ho
Response (the group): Repeats the above
Call: What d'ya say, What d'ya know.
Response: Repeats the above
Call: I got the _____ _____ boogey. *(Child who is greeting fills in the blank with two adjectives. For example, "the wet wild boogey," "the jumpin' jive boogey," "the flap happy boogey," etc.)*

Response: He/She's got the _____ _____ boogey.

Call: And I got it right now.

Response: He/She's got it right now.

Call: I'm gonna pick it on up. *(Child pretends to pick something up.)*

Response: He/She's gonna pick it on up.

Call: And pass it on along. *(Child pretends to pass an object to the next child in circle.)*

Response: Repeats the above.

Call: To my good friend _____. *(Child fills in with the name of the child who is being handed the "boogey".)*

Response: To his/her good friend _____.

Call: And she's/he's got it right now.

Response: Repeats the above.

Appendix E

Morning Meeting Activities

The following are good non-competitive activities to use in Morning Meeting. There are calm activities, boisterous activities, serious activities, and silly activities. Many provide practice with communication and thinking skills and can be easily adapted to fit the skill-level of your class.

Each activity has a suggested age span.

Some activities are marked with a ▣ These are especially good to use at the beginning of the year. They are fairly easy to teach, help children learn each others' names, and build a sense of community.

Many of these activities are selected from the following books that focus on non-competitive activities and fun, but peaceful, play.

Everyone Wins! Sambhava and Josette Luvmour. 1990. New Society Publishers.

The Friendly Classroom for a Small Planet. Gretchen Bodenhamer, Leonard Burger, Priscilla Prutzman and Lee Stern. 1988. New Society Publishers.

Keeping the Peace: Practicing Cooperation and Conflict Resolution with Preschoolers. Susanne Wichert. 1989. New Society Publishers.

These excellent resources for teachers are available directly from New Society Publishers, PO Box 189, Gabriola Island, BC, VOR 1XO, Canada. Phone: 1-800-567-6772. www.newsociety.com.

"Keeping the Peace" Activity Ideas

The following activities are taken from *Keeping the Peace: Practicing Cooperation and Conflict Resolution with Preschoolers.* Susanne Wichert. 1989. New Society Publishers. Used with permission. To order, call 1-800-567-6772.

Clapping Names (PreK–3) ▣

Procedure: The object is to clap one beat for each syllable in a child's name. Start with an explanation that different names have different numbers of syllables and you can clap to the syllables while chanting the name. I generally start with my own name and ask children if they would like their name done. Clap once for each syllable while chanting the name. Generally, children will spontaneously join in with you. If not, encourage them to do so. The activity can be varied by clapping loudly or softly.

Comments: This is a good activity for learning names in a new group or if there is a new child in the group. This can also be a good way to learn last names.

Hot and Cold (K–6th)

Procedure: This game has probably been around as long as children have and can be a wonderful vehicle for bonding a group. It is essential that the adult monitor carefully and intervene so there is no failure. This involves abstract concepts and can be difficult for young children to grasp. You will need to do some preparatory work before doing the game with the group.

An object is selected that will be hidden. The adult should outline any areas that will be off-limits. Explain that the object will be hidden and a player must seek it out. The job of the group is to guide the seeker by saying "hot" if he's getting near, and "cold" if he is moving away from the object. If there are two adults available, it may be a good idea to have one of the adults be the first seeker. The other adult can then guide the rest of the group in giving direction.

The seeker is sent out of the room while the object is hidden. You should attempt to get group agreement to choose the hiding place. Do not make it too difficult, as the attempt is not to frustrate the seeker, rather to work in unison with the person to help them find the object. When the object has been stashed, the seeker comes back into the room and begins the search. The group verbally guides the seeker to the hiding place. Attempt to structure your time so that everyone who wishes can have a turn.

Cooperative Spider Web (PreK–Adult)

Materials: Ball of string, area large enough for children to sit in a circle.

Procedure: Explain to children that you are going to make a giant spider web, but that this will only work if everyone does their job. Have children sit in a circle. The circle should be fairly small so children can roll the ball of string to each other.

Start with one child, handing him the end of the string and the ball. He should use one hand to hang onto the end and the other hand to hold the ball. This child then rolls the ball to another child in the circle, who holds onto the string with one hand while rolling the ball to another child. Continue in this manner.

You may have to remind children frequently to hold on, because if everyone doesn't hold the string the entire web will collapse. Don't worry if children occasionally roll the ball to the person sitting next to them. Continued movement of the string will ultimately result in a web.

Comments: The first few times, the adult may wish to remain outside of the circle in order to help children continue to hold and/or to help the ball of yarn reach its destination. It is sometimes possible to have a discussion of some real life instances in which everyone must do their part or things don't work well. I've found that a heavier string works better than a very thin one.

"The Friendly Classroom" Activity Ideas

The following activities are taken from *The Friendly Classroom for a Small Planet*. Gretchen Bodenhamer, Leonard Burger, Priscilla Prutzman and Lee Stern. 1988. New Society Publishers. Used with permission. To order, call 1-800-567-6772.

Introductory Name Game (PreK–Adult) ▣

Have everyone sit in a circle to foster group feeling and to allow everyone to see and pay attention to the person speaking. Ask a simple, interesting question: "What is your favorite dessert? What is a sport you enjoy? What is your favorite soup?" Go around the circle and have everyone say his or her name and answer the question. Participation should be voluntary; some people may choose not to answer the question. At the beginning, questions shouldn't be too personal. Children often prefer to talk about things that are outside of school.

The Memory Name Game (K–Adult) ▣

The Memory Name Game is more challenging. It is fairly easy to do if children already know each other. The structure is the same as that used in the Introductory Name Game except that children are asked to repeat what each person before them has replied. It is important to ask just one simple question, such as "What is your favorite food?" so that the last person in the circle has a chance of remembering and repeating what everyone else has said. Since there is much repetition, this is an excellent exercise for not only remembering names, but also for learning about each person in a group.

The Introduce-Your-Neighbor Game (K–Adult) ▣

The Introduce-Your-Neighbor Game helps people learn something about others in a group. Have everyone sit in a circle. Ask people to form pairs and then take turns talking about themselves. Be sure to announce the half-time mark after two or three minutes, at which time the other person in the pair takes a turn. Then have everyone return to the large circle to introduce his or her partner to the whole group. It is preferable to have people introduce partners voluntarily since this involves more direct participation. If this is awkward, go around the circle for introductions.

For people who prefer more structure, ask a specific question such as "What are three things you like to do?" Give people a chance to think for a minute and then ask them to form pairs. Examples are helpful for getting people started: "In the summer I like to ride horses. In the winter I like to lie in the snow."

Three Question Interview (2nd–Adult) ⬛

Three Question Interview is a technique which helps people to learn several things about participants. This is especially effective in a group of parents or teachers who don't know each other well, though it can also be used with children and adults who are familiar with each other. Provide each person with paper and pencil. Have the participants form pairs, preferably with someone they don't know very well. They are to ask each other three simple questions, such as "What is a movie you enjoyed recently?" or "What is one place you would like to visit?" The person asking the questions can jot down his partner's responses. When both people have had a chance to ask three questions, they find other partners and repeat the process.

After fifteen to twenty minutes, or when each person has had a chance to interview several others, everyone returns to the large circle. The facilitator goes around the circle and for each person says, "This is _____. What do people know about _____?" People who interviewed that person share what they learned, either from memory or by referring to their notes. Allow time for each person to have a turn. This is an especially affirming exercise for introducing people to each other.

Human Protractor (PreK–4th)

Have everyone stand in a large circle with hands touching toes. While counting from one to twenty, children gradually raise their arms so that by twenty, their hands are reaching towards the sky. Tell children to remember where their hands were at different numbers. Then call out numbers between one and twenty while the group assumes the position for each number. Children love leading this energizing game. It builds community because everyone does the same thing together. For younger children (PreK and K), use it as a counting game and call it One-to-Ten *(see following activity)*.

"One-to-Ten" Math Game (K–6th)

Instead of calling out numbers as in Human Protractor *(previous activity)*, the leader calls out addition and subtraction problems. For example, the leader calls out "ten minus two." The others respond "eight" and assume that position. You can play this game using whatever range of numbers are most appropriate for the group. It turns math lessons into fun and group-building activities. Rotate the leader so everyone receives affirmation from the group.

Pantomime This Object (PreK–3rd) ▣

Young children especially like this game. Choose a real object, such as a broom, and use it to pantomime something else: a guitar, a horse, a violin, etc. Then pass the object around the circle and have children pantomime something with it. Children come up with endless variations. The pantomimed objects are fun to guess, and the game affirms the one taking a turn. Be sure the object you choose has enough possibilities.

Occupation Pantomime (2nd–Adult)

Children take turns pantomiming an occupation while others guess what the occupation is. Describe this game by pantomiming an occupation rather than explaining it verbally. The game builds confidence and unifies the group as everyone's attention is focused on each child in turn. The game complements a unit on occupations and helps children build their vocabularies.

Zoom (1st–Adult)

Zoom is a large circle game which encourages laughter. Imagine the sound of a racing car—zoom! Start by saying *zoom* and turning your head quickly to either side of the circle. The person on that side passes the *zoom* to the next person, and so on until everyone has passed the *zoom* around the circle. Next explain that the word *eek* makes the car stop and reverse direction; whenever *eek* is said, the *zoom* goes the opposite way around the circle.

At first it is helpful to allow only one *eek* per person to prevent the *eeks* and *zooms* from concentrating in one area of the circle. Later, try discarding the rule and encouraging cooperation by making the children responsible for getting the *zoom* all the way around the circle. If the group isn't too large, it is a good idea to continue the game until everyone has had a chance to say *eek*, otherwise everyone who did not say *eek* can do it together.

My Bonnie (PreK–Adult)

Everyone sings the song "My Bonnie Lies Over the Ocean." Whenever words beginning with a "b" are sung, children alternate between sitting and standing. For example:

My Bonnie *(stand)* lies over the ocean

My Bonnie *(sit)* lies over the sea

This game is very active; some children may not be able to finish the song or keep up with the rapid sitting and standing. It is so silly that it gets people laughing right away, serving as a good energizer and tension reliever.

The Telephone Game (PreK–3rd)

The Telephone Game usually highlights problems in communication. The message received by the last person differs from the original in an amusing way. When this game is used to improve listening skills, it is played in a different way. The goal is to have the last child receive the original message accurately by analyzing how messages get around. Sit in a circle and begin with a simple sentence, such as "Last night the moon was shining and I loved watching it." Pass the message around the room in a whisper. More likely than not, it will be garbled by the time it reaches the last child. Ask children what helps them to hear the message correctly. Answers may include speaking into the listener's ear, speaking slowly and clearly, a quiet room, etc. List children's answers on the blackboard.

Think of a new message and go around the circle again. Make the length and difficulty of the message appropriate for the group. If the final message differs from the original, resume the discussion using the list generated earlier. Go around the circle a third time and tell children to check back if the message is unclear. They may ask, "Did you say _____?" and the other child may reply, "Yes, I said _____." Checking back should enable children to pass around the message successfully. This game is a group-building way to improve children's listening skills.

Telegraph (K–Adult)

Telegraph is similar to the Telephone Game except that the message is nonverbal and instead consists of squeezes and pauses sent through the hands. Have children close their eyes so no one can see the message. Children hold hands in a circle, which makes this game a unifying experience. After the message goes around the circle, the last child explains verbally what it was. The message can also be sent in both directions until one child receives it from both sides, especially in large groups. You can use Telegraph with a history unit and have children pretend to send a message from New York to

California and back. Another variation is to send messages using the Morse code. This game is also known as "Electricity."

The Description Game (2nd–Adult)

The Description Game encourages children to listen closely to each other. Have three children give different descriptions of the same object without naming it. The object described should be fairly complex and visible to everyone else. Have the rest of the class use the three descriptions to identify the object. A bulletin board, for example, may be described as something with pictures or writing on it. Some descriptions may be general, others very specific. The Description Game improves listening skills by encouraging children to concentrate on what others say. It is also an observation game which teaches children to focus on the details of an object. The Description Game can lead to a discussion of how everyone sees things differently. You can also use it as a creative writing exercise.

Pantomime One Thing You Like to Do (2nd–Adult) ▣

Pantomime One Thing You Like to Do is group building and personally affirming. In a circle, ask children to pantomime one thing they like to do. Be sure to let each person finish the pantomime before others start to guess. Everyone who wants to do a pantomime should have a chance.

Magic Box (2nd–Adult)

Magic Box is another pantomime game. Place an imaginary magic box in the center of the circle. Each child in turn goes to the box and takes out something, pantomiming an activity or game. When others in the circle guess the activity, they go to the center and join in, and the originator tells them if they are correct. Another child takes something out of the box, and the process continues. The game affirms those in the center of the circle.

"Everyone Wins!" Activity Ideas

The following activities are taken from *Everyone Wins!* Sambhava and Josette Luvmour. 1990. New Society Publishers. Used with permission. To order, call 1-800-567-6772.

How Many Are Standing? (PreK–4th) B

Sit in a circle. Anyone stands up whenever they want to, but cannot remain standing longer than five seconds. Aim of the game is to have exactly four standing at one time.

Variations: Vary group size and amount standing or time standing up.

Special Hints: Great for an icebreaker and for the little ones.

What Did I Do? (K–Adult) B

Group examines one child in the center of the circle. That child then leaves the circle and without being seen by the group changes one thing about her appearance. The child then returns to the circle and others try to guess what has been changed.

Variations: Vary the time of observation and/or the amount of things changed (5 or 6 things). Do it with an area and not a person. Do it with partners.

Special Hints: Don't let it become competitive.

Coseeki/Follow the Leader (PreK–Adult) B

One player goes where she cannot see the others. A leader is chosen. She does a movement which the others follow. The leader changes movement regularly. The others follow the leader's movement. The hidden one returns and by watching everyone tries to guess who the leader is.

Variations: Send more than one away and have them confer. Limit the guesses. Have two leaders and switch off movements. Use movements that make no sound.

Special Hints: Join the fun!

Where Is It? (2nd–Adult)

Materials: pebble

In a circle, one player is in the middle with eyes closed. Others pass the pebble. The one in the middle opens his/her eyes and tries to guess who has the stone. Others keep passing it or pretend they are passing it. The pebble must always be in motion. Passes and fakes go on in both directions but always between persons next to one another.

Variations: Place a ring on a string that is long enough to go all the way around the inside of the circle. Children hold the string with both hands and pass the ring or pretend to pass the ring to each other.

Special Hints: Encourage good fakery.

Responsive Classroom Favorites

The following activities are Responsive Classroom favorites, gathered over the years from classrooms across the country.

Pop (K–4th)

The meeting leader/line leader or teacher chooses a number such as 5. Going around the circle, the children count, 1, 2, 3, 4, until they get to the designated number. The fifth child in the circle then pops up and says, "Pop." This goes around and around until everyone in the circle is standing. Variations include "popping" for even numbers, odd numbers, multiples of 2, 5, etc.

The Cold Wind Blows (K–Adult) ▣

This activity is a great way for children to learn about each other and to see what they have in common with classmates. Every person, except for one, needs to have a clearly marked spot in the circle (a chair, a book on the floor, etc.). One person starts in the middle and makes a statement such as "The cold wind blows for anyone

who loves cats." Everyone who has a cat walks into the middle of
the circle and then quickly finds a new spot to sit around the circle. There are two rules for finding a new spot: You can't go back
to the same spot and you can't go to the spot immediately to the
left or right of your old spot. One person will end up without a
spot and will stay in the middle to make the next statement: "The
cold wind blows for anyone who plays the piano or likes to play
soccer or has an older brother, etc."

It's important to stress that players name categories related to
people's interests and backgrounds and not just their clothing or
appearance. It may be helpful, especially with younger children, to
brainstorm a list of possible statements before the game begins.

Broomstick (K–Adult)

One child goes into the middle of the circle and uses a stick to
mime something (a baseball player, a person with a metal detector,
etc.). The person who guesses correctly can either go into the center next or call on another child who would like a turn.

Category Snap (1st–Adult)

The group sits in a circle in such a way that they can slap their own
knees. A category is chosen such as fruits. The leader starts the
rhythm which is some combination of a knee slap, hand clap and
ending with a right-hand finger snap, and then a left-hand finger
snap (in the beginning or with younger children, it might be easier to use two knee slaps and two hand claps before going to the finger snaps). The leader begins by announcing the category on the
right-hand finger snap and naming one of the elements with the
left-hand finger snap. The next person in line is doing the rhythm
with everybody else but must be ready to name the leader's fruit
with the right-hand finger snap and then a new element in that
same category with the left-hand finger snap. The play continues as
so around the circle. Once an element has been named it cannot be
used again.

Variation: Each person at the beginning of the game chooses an element of the category to be theirs. The leader begins the game by identifying his/her own element with the right hand finger snap and then names another player's element with the left hand finger snap. This variation sends the action jumping around the circle and demands that children not only listen but also remember other player's elements.

Beach Ball Math (1–6)

The group has a beach ball with a number written on each panel, including the small circles at the top and bottom. The Meeting leader begins by choosing either addition, subtraction, multiplication, or division (depending on the skill level of the group) and tossing the ball to someone. The person who catches the ball looks at the numbers beneath his/her hands and tries to solve the equation, requesting help if needed. The child then tosses the ball to someone else in the circle.

Description Game: A Variation on Twenty Questions (2nd–Adult)

The group sits in a circle and tapes a card on one person's back with a word written on it that names a person, place, or thing (or any category of study that the class is engaged in—fish, mountains, rivers, capitals, children in the class). The child with the card on can ask up to ten yes-or-no questions to try to determine what is written on his/her back. Each time a question is asked the class responds with thumbs up or down. The game is like twenty questions. The teacher can designate certain questions or types of questions as not allowed in a particular game to increase the difficulty. The game can also be played in teams. The child can make a guess at any time with a maximum of 3 guesses. After 10 questions, the child can ask for clues from the audience before a final guess.

Guess the Number (2nd–Adult)

This game helps children develop questioning skills, listening skills, and cooperative thinking skills. To start, the teacher thinks of a number between 1 and 50, writes it down on a piece of paper and keeps the paper hidden until the number is guessed. Sitting in a circle, one at a time, going around the circle, each student takes a turn, asking a "yes or no" question to determine the number. If a student does not have a question, she may "pass."

Encourage students to think of questions that will give them information about the number, rather than questions that just eliminate one number. Instead of asking if it's the number after 14, for example, students might ask if it is a two-digit number, whether it's larger than 10, or if it has a 5 in it. A student who thinks she knows the number may take a guess, but if the guess is incorrect, the guessing continues.

When the number is finally guessed correctly, the teacher may choose another number or pick a child to do this. In order to emphasize the cooperative nature of this game, it is important that the child who finally guessed the number is not the next one to choose a number. The new round of questioning begins with the child whose turn was after the child who guessed the number in the previous game. The ultimate goal of this game is to see how many numbers the group, working cooperatively, can figure out within a certain period of time.

Variation: Choose a number range that appropriately challenges the age and skill level of the group of students.

Improv (2nd–Adult)

This is a theater warm-up exercise that can be very entertaining and can help children feel comfortable with acting. Two people go to the center of the circle and start acting out a simple scene such as eating at a restaurant, doing homework together at school, etc. At any point, someone from the circle can call out "freeze." The two people freeze while the person who called out goes into the center and takes the place of one of the actors by putting his/her body in the exact same position. The two in the center now act out a different scene that makes sense for the positions that they are starting in.

What Are You Doing? (2nd–Adult)

Another good theater warm-up exercise. In this activity, one person begins the game by miming some simple action in the center of the circle such as brushing one's hair. The next person in the circle approaches the hair-brusher and asks, "What are you doing?" The hair-brusher responds by saying something completely different such as "I'm washing the floor." The person who asked now pretends that he/she is washing the floor. The next person from the circle then comes to ask the floor-washer, "What are you doing?" This goes on until everyone in the circle has had a chance to mime an action.

Match-Up (2nd–Adult)

Materials: scissors, paper, marker

Print a short nursery rhyme, poem, or song on a sheet of paper. Duplicate the page and cut it into strips with one line on each strip. Distribute one strip to each child. Tell the children they will find others who have the same line by standing and repeating their line. After the children have formed groups, do a complete reading of the nursery rhyme, starting with the group who has the first line. A sample nursery rhyme to use might be:

Jack and Jill went up the hill
To fetch a pail of water.
Jack fell down and broke his crown
And Jill came tumbling after.

Variation: Choose a poem from your reading book or a song the children are learning in music class.

Category Circle (2nd–Adult)

Children stand or sit in a circle. One child goes into the center with a ball (nerf, bean bag, anything easy to catch and pass). The child in the center turns around three times, stops and tosses the ball to someone standing across from him/her. The child who catches the ball names a category and immediately starts passing the ball to the person on the right who continues passing the ball. The child in the center tries to name as many items in the category as possible before the ball is passed all the way around to the child who started the category. Another child can be assigned to count how many items in the category are named.

Pica Fermé Nada (2nd–adult)

This is a cooperative strategy game that can be played with the whole class. A person leads and starts the game by thinking of a number with an agreed upon number of digits (the number of digits is based on the age and experience of the children playing) and then writes that number on a piece of paper which is put aside until the end of the game. For our demonstration example we will say the number is 386—a number with three digits.

Next the leader writes a blank for each digit of the number on a piece of chart paper or on the blackboard like this: _ _ _ (i.e., three blanks for the three digits of 386). The object of the game is for the rest of the class to work together to figure out the number by suggesting other three digit numbers. Each child has the opportunity to give a suggestion for a three digit number as turns are taken one at a time in progression around the circle. A child also has the option to pass if they do not want to suggest a number.

Each time a number is suggested, the leader responds to that number with information about whether the numerals in the suggested number are actually in the "mystery" number or not, and whether they are in the right digit place. The information is provided in the following format:

- *Pica (abbrev. = P)* means the numeral is in the "mystery" number but it is not in the correct place

- *Fermé (abbrev. = F)* means the numeral and place are correct

- *Nada (abbrev. = N)* means the numeral is not in the mystery number at all

For example, if someone suggested 365 for the mystery number 386, the leader would write beside 365—F P N. Then the next person in the circle would take their turn to suggest a number based on the information gathered from the previous number which confirmed that the mystery number has no 5 in it, has a 3 in it in the hundreds place and finally has a 6 in it but not in the tens place.

The game continues in this fashion until someone is ready to actually name the number. In order to name the number, the child must be ready to explain the thinking that solved the mystery number. To help build a cooperative spirit to the game, the rules allow that a child may ask for strategic thinking before he or she suggests a number and that the other children may ask permission of the child who is about to take a turn to offer strategic thinking to them. However, the child, whose turn it is, is not obliged to ask for or to give permission for strategic thinking.

For younger children or for older children just learning the game, the symbols P F N are given in direct relation to the placement of the digits of the number. In 365 the F was given first in direct relation to the 3 in the hundreds place and the P was given second in direct relation to the 6 in the tens place. When children are able to quickly and easily guess the mystery number in this fashion, it is time to change the way in which the information about the numerals is provided.

The more challenging way to play is when the Pica, Fermé and Nada symbols are given with no direct relationship to the placement of the numerals in the suggested number. For example with 365 the symbols are given N F P and if the next suggested number

was 357 the symbols might be given as N F N. The random placement of the symbols makes the strategic thinking all the more challenging and fun.

Hands Up for '99 (change for correct year) (3rd–Adult)

The teacher names a category and a child who will start the first
round of the activity. Once children know the activity, they can
name the category and start the round. Each child names something that fits in the category. The naming moves one-by-one
around the circle. If a child misses by repeating or taking more than
a few seconds, the activity starts over again with the child next in
the circle. The object is to get all the way around the circle without a miss.

Hands up / / *(silent beats)*

For '99 / / *(silent beats)*

Gonna' name *(clap, clap)*

Some _____*(clap, clap)* *(A category is named, such as rivers, states,
animals, etc.)*

One apiece *(clap, clap)*

No repeats *(clap, clap)*

No hesitation *(clap, clap)*

No duplication *(clap, clap)*

Starting with *(clap, clap)*

_____ *(Fill in with child's name and child says something that
fits in the category.)*

Ra-de-o (Radio) (3rd–Adult)

The class forms a circle with room to form another circle on the
outside as the game progresses. Each syllable of the world "Ra-de-
o" has a specific arm and hand gesture that goes with it and deter-
mines where the action will be sent next. One person starts by saying, "Ra" and puts either their left hand or their right hand above
their head pointing to the person on either the left or right side of

them. That person says the next syllable, "de" and puts either their left or their right hand under their chin pointing to either the person on their left or their right side. The next person says the last syllable, "o" and points to anyone in the circle who then starts the action all over again by saying, "Ra." The object of the game is to listen, be aware and think about which action and syllable is needed, and not make a mistake.

If a player does make a mistake, they come out of the inner circle and begin to form the circle of "hecklers" who are on the outside of the inner circle. The hecklers have a very important job. They are to use words and sounds to try to distract the other players so that they cannot concentrate on the actions of the game. Hecklers may not stand in front of players or use their arms or hands to obstruct the players. Instead they may talk incessantly in a player's ear; they may sing at the top of their lungs; they may tell jokes or stories, etc. Pretty soon most players are on the outside heckling and there are very few on the inside trying to pass the action. Again, the game can be ended before it gets down to the last player.

Alibi (3rd–Adult)

One person is chosen as the detective and leaves the room. While the detective is out, a leader decides on a crime that has been committed and chooses one person to be the guilty party. The groups sits in a circle and the detective is invited back to the room. The leader tells the detective what crime has occurred. Now the detective asks each player in the circle for their alibi—"Where were you at the time of the crime?" Going around the circle in order, each player gives an alibi. The detective listens carefully and then asks for the alibis again. Going around the circle in the same order as before, each player must give the exact same alibi using the exact same words except for the child who was chosen as the guilty party. The guilty party changes their alibi just slightly. For example, the first time perhaps the guilty one said, "I was at the doctor's."

And the second time the guilty one says, "I was at the dentist's." The detective gets three attempts to guess who the guilty person is and then a new detective is chosen.

Aunt Minerva (4th–Adult)

A leader decides on a category and does not tell anyone else. Instead the leader gives several examples to demonstrate the category by telling things that Aunt Minerva likes and doesn't like. For example, if the category was hot and cold, the leader might say, "Aunt Minerva likes Florida but doesn't like Alaska. Aunt Minerva likes heavy down quilts but doesn't like thin sheets. Aunt Minerva likes soup but doesn't like ice cream." The other players try to figure out the category and when they think they have, they give an example of something Aunt Minerva likes and doesn't like to show their idea. The leader acknowledges whether the guesser is right or not about what Aunt Minerva likes and doesn't like. The leader keeps giving examples and listening to others guesses until many of the children have the category. However, a new round should be started before there are only three or four children left.

The Fruit Game (4th–Adult) ◼

Here's a fun ice-breaking activity which older children enjoy. Go around the circle and have each person name a piece of fruit with no repeats. From this point on everyone covers their teeth with their lips, the object of the game being to not show your teeth. One person begins the game by saying their own fruit followed by another person's fruit, such as "banana/mango," without showing any teeth. Then, the person who is the mango has to say his or her fruit, plus one other, such as "mango/grapefruit," and so on. It is very difficult for children not to laugh and show their teeth in this activity. If someone does show their teeth, they simply watch the game which is almost as much fun. The game has no definitive end; you may want to start with a time limit so that it doesn't go on too long.

Caught Red-Handed (4th–Adult)

In this activity, there are two or three (or more) small objects that get passed around the room. One person leaves the circle or closes his/her eyes for a moment as the objects begin to be passed around. The person then returns, stands in the circle, and tries to figure out where the objects are in the circle. The students in the circle pass the objects around as sneakily as possible as well as pretend to be passing an object when they're not. At all times students should either be faking a pass or actually passing an object. The person in the middle is allowed three guesses for the whereabouts of each object. These guesses should be made quickly in order to keep the game moving along.

Encore (5th–Adult)

A fun and quick game which calls for teamwork. Divide the group into several teams based on where children are sitting in the circle. The teacher calls out a word or topic (examples: rain, rivers, dancing, farm animals, etc.) and each team tries to come up with as many songs as they can within a given time (5 minutes is plenty) that use that topic or word.

The Pattern Game (5th–Adult)

While older children love the trickery and detective skills involved in this activity, it does require careful modeling and a sizable chunk of time in order to be played well. The game begins with one person going out of the room while the rest of the group decides on a pattern for how they will answer questions. Here are some examples of patterns which the group might choose: everyone will answer for the person to their left; everyone will answer for one person in the circle; everyone will answer for the person who is asking the questions. Once the pattern is set, the child returns to the room and begins to ask questions of individuals in an effort to figure out the pattern. The child might ask questions like, "Are you wearing sneakers?" "Are you a girl?" "Does your name begin with M?" The best kinds of questions are yes or no questions which the questioner already knows the answer to. The questioner should also be encouraged to ask questions rapidly and to as many people as possible.

Sometimes the questioner will ask a person a question which they do not know the answer to. For example, if everyone is answering for Claire and the questioner asks, "Do you have a brother?" there will be some people who do not know the answer to this. If you are asked a question which you do not know the answer to you must venture a guess anyway. If you answer incorrectly, anyone in the group who knows the true answer will at that point call out, "Pattern!" As you can imagine, the job of the questioner can be very challenging. You may want to have two people working together as questioners to make it a bit easier. This is a good activity to save until later in the year when your students know each other well.

Additional Resources

Here are a few additional excellent resources for cooperative games and activities. These can be ordered through Northeast Foundation for Children, 1-800-360-6332.

Cooperative Sports & Games Book I. 1978. Terry Orlick. New York: Pantheon.

Cooperative Sports & Games Book II. 1988. Terry Orlick. New York: Pantheon.

The Incredible Indoor Games Book. 1982. Bob Gregson. Carthage, IL: Fearon Teacher Aids.

Appendix F

Samples of News and Announcements Charts

Key:

- Words that are in *italics* change each day.

- <u>Underlined parts</u> are what might be left blank for the class to fill in at Meeting or for individuals to fill in before Meeting begins.

Pre-kindergarten

Beginning of the Year:

Good Morning!
Laura is first.
Raymond is the doorholder.
Today is *Monday.*
We will fingerpaint.

Middle of the Year:

Good Morning!
Thomas is first.
Maria is the doorholder.
Today is *Thursday.*
Do you like pizza? ❏ *Yes* ❏ *No*

Kindergarten

Beginning of the Year:

Good Day!
Laura is first.
Raymond is the doorholder.
Today is *Monday, October 4, 1999.*
We will fingerpaint.
What colors do you like?

Middle of the Year:

Good Day, Children!
Thomas is _irst.
Maria is the _oorholder.
_oday is _ _ _ _ _ _ _ _,
February _ _, _ _ _ _.
We will write a story about our
trip to the store. Draw a food
that you saw at the store.
Tameka's word is: _ _ _ _ _ _ _ _

First Grade

Beginning of the Year:

Dear Children,

Laura _ _ first.

Raymond _ _ the doorholder.

Today is _ _ _ _ _ _ _ _ _,

October _, _ _ _ _.

We will talk about our spider
today. Can you tell one thing
you observed about our spider?

Luis' secret word is: _ _ _ _ _ _

Middle of the Year:

Good Morning, *Mathematicians!*

Thomas is _ _ _ st.

Maria is the doorhold_ _.

Today is **Th** _ _ **sday,**

_ _ _ _ _ _ _ _, _ _, _ _ _ _.

Here is a math challenge for today:

$4+4+2+2=$

Write your answer here.

Tameka's secret message is:

_ _ _ _ _ _ _ _ _

Second Grade

Beginning of the Year:

Good Morning, *Friendly Workers*
Today is _____, _____ __, ___.
Laura is first and *Raymond* is our Greeting leader
Yesterday we talked about how to invite someone
to join in an activity with you today we will practice
how to do this who remembers some friendly actions
that you might use write your ideas here
What's wrong with this message?
Luis' secret message says

— — — — — — — — — — —

— — — — — — — — — —

Middle of the Year:

Good Morning, *Authors:*
Today is _____, _____ __, ___.
The shortcut way to write the date is
__ / __ / __.
Laura is first and *Raymond* is our Greeting leader.
You and your partner will be given a special place to
read. After you read, what are some questions you can
ask your partner to help you talk about your story? Each
of you will have a partner that you will read to. We will
be reading our published books to the kindergartners
after lunch.

Third–Sixth Grades

Beginning of the Year

Dear *Friendly Workers,*
Today is *Monday, October 4, 1999.*
Laura will lead our Greeting.
Our sharing this week is "Baby <u>Memories.</u>" If you are signing up, remember to share a memory about you when you were a baby.
Tomorrow we will start to do our "New Friend" interviews. Here are some ideas to think about:
What is an interview?
Why are we doing interviews?
What <u>might</u> be a good interview question?
Look at the underlined words.
Be ready to tell how many syllables are in each one.

Middle of the Year:

Dear *Awesome Scholars,*
Today is *February 9, 1999* (_ _/ _ _/ _ _) and *Thomas* will lead our Greeting.
The illustrations you did for our class read aloud story are fantastic! The ideas they show are all so different. I want to display them all. Who would like to plan and arrange the display? We are working on some math challenges today. Here's one sample for you to try:
2,435 - 1,569 = _____. Be ready to tell what you did to solve it.
Syllable challenge: Choose a word for us to tell how many syllables.

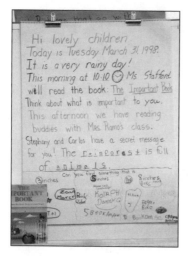

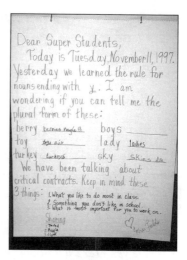

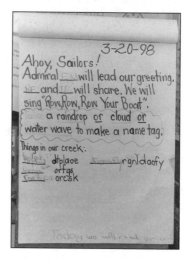

A sampling of News and Announcements Charts

Appendix G

Suggestions for Creating News
and Announcements Charts

*The following suggestions illustrate the many possibilities and variations
that exist for creating News and Announcements charts.*

Special Topics

Some teachers plan their messages in the following way in order to
vary content and also to give a predictable routine.

Monday: Weekend

Think of one thing you did over the weekend that was fun . . .
interesting . . . challenging . . . exciting . . . hard . . . etc.

Dear Class,
Welcome back. I hope you had a good weekend. Check below if
you had fun doing the following:

- ☐ Read a good book or saw a good movie
- ☐ Played a fun game
- ☐ Went to a new place
- ☐ Played sports
- ☐ Visited with friends
- ☐ Other

Tuesday: Math

Make up problems from real life situations, surveys, and classroom
curriculum:
If we order pizza for our class party and everyone gets 2 slices, how
many pizzas do we need? (What other information do you need to
solve this problem?)

Survey: Check below if you have a pet. What fraction of our class does not have a pet?

__dogs __cats __birds __gerbils __other

Wednesday: Humor

Riddles, jokes, cartoons, doodles...

> *Hey, Class . . .*
> *What?*
> *What do you do with a blue elephant ???*
> *We don't know.*
> *Try to cheer him up !!!*

(May leave out answer and take guesses.)

Thursday: Language Arts

Use word games, poetry, songs, unscrambling words, similes, "book reviews," introduce a new game, twenty questions, etc.

"Madam I'm Adam." Reverse each word. Now what does it say? How many other words can you think of that are the same whether you write them left to right or right to left?
List your ideas below:

Friday: Current Events

Use headlines, articles, pictures, newspaper, etc. to initiate a discussion about relevant news. May also lead to class debates about ongoing issues, such as building electric cars, etc.

Elements

The Morning Message can include many of the following elements:

1. *A friendly greeting—Dear Students, Dear Fine Fifth Graders, Good Morning, Cooperative Class, etc.*

2. *An item that names or describes students and/or asks for an informed guess. Keep these upbeat, welcoming, and fun.*

   Some examples:

   - "Class Riddles"—Ask questions based on information about students or their projects:
     Who likes to draw?
     Who just had a birthday?
     Who has a new puppy?
     Who has the middle name "Rose?"

   - Fun tallies:
     Check what you did this weekend
     ❏ Visited a relative
     ❏ Played a game
     ❏ Went to a movie
     ❏ Other

     (Others tallies might include a check for your favorite kind of book, favorite time of day, favorite comfort, favorite object, etc.)

   - Morning Meeting or class responsibilities:
     James will lead sharing today.
     _____ will lead the activity.
     _____ will present a current events report.
     _____ has a birthday today.

   - Fun informational questions or puzzles:
     Where do you think the coldest place in the U.S. was this weekend? Check below.
     ❏ Nome, Alaska
     ❏ Cheyenne, Wyoming
     ❏ Orlando, Florida

3. An interactive task—a chance for students to respond (briefly) in writing on the chart.
Some examples:

- Write one word that describes how you felt about your day yesterday.

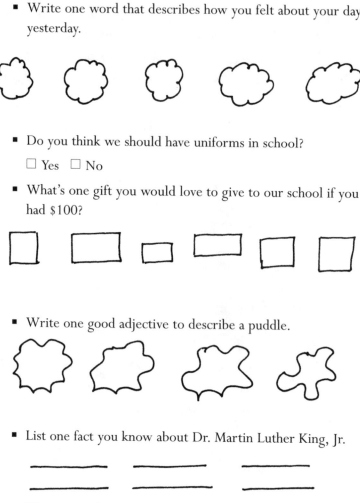

- Do you think we should have uniforms in school?
  ☐ Yes   ☐ No

- What's one gift you would love to give to our school if you had $100?

- Write one good adjective to describe a puddle.

- List one fact you know about Dr. Martin Luther King, Jr.

- Write one adjective that describes a good friend.

- Between 1 and 10, how many prime (or odd or even) numbers are there? List your guess below.

4. **An important piece of news or reminder about the day:**

   - We will have a visitor from _____.

   - We will review division. Who remembers what $\overline{)}$ means?

   - We need to remember our rule for keeping recess safe and fun. Think of one way that you will keep it safe.

   - Bring your writing to Meeting today. Be prepared to share a favorite message.

5. **A direction (often administrative):**

   - Put your homework in the red bin.

   - Put your trip permission slips in the envelope by the clock.

   - Remember to sign up for projects.

6. **Practice skills. This is not a time to introduce skills. It is a time to model, practice, and encourage peer learning. It is a lively, short warm-up:**

   - Vocabulary—encourage use of context (Dear Studious Students, Considerate People, Cantankerous Class)

   - Punctuation

   - Leave out all periods. Students will show where they belong.

   - Make mistakes and have class fix them (May 4. 1999).

   - Write silly conversations to practice quotation marks. (Teacher said stand on your head. I'd be happy to said the student.)

   - Spelling

- Fixing teacher's mistakes (We wer late for recesse . . .)
- Homonyms (Deer Students, Eye sea a lot of . . .)
- Scramble words from spelling list for students to unscramble.
- Fill in blanks (co_nt_y).
- Math
- Word problem of the week
- Date equations (16 equations for November 16th)
- If you had $18.00 to spend for the class, what would you buy? (Move decimals: If you had $.18 . . .)
- Attendance math: What fraction of class is absent/present?

REFERENCES

Berman, Sheldon. 1998. Keynote Address at Responsive Leadership Institute, July 13, at Northeast Foundation for Children, Greenfield, Massachusetts.

Charney, Ruth S., Marlynn K. Clayton, Chip Wood. 1996. *Guidelines for The Responsive Classroom* (Training Manual). Greenfield, Massachusetts: Northeast Foundation for Children.

Elias, Maurice J., Joseph E. Zins, Roger P. Weissberg, Karin S. Frey, Mark T. Greenberg, Norris M. Haynes, Rachael Kessler, Mary E. Schwab-Stone, Timothy P. Shriver. 1997. *Promoting Social and Emotional Learning: Guidelines for Educators.* Alexandria, Virginia: Association for Supervision and Curriculum Development.

Fraser, Jane and Donna Skolnick. 1994. *On Their Way: Celebrating Second Graders as They Read and Write.* Portsmouth, New Hampshire: Heinemann.

Goldsmith, Suzanne. Quoted in Glenda Valentine. 1998. "Don't Walk Away." *Teaching Tolerance* (Spring): 4.

Ilg, Francis L., M.D., Louise Bates Ames, Ph.D., Sidney M. Baker, M.D. 1981 (Revised Edition). *Child Behavior.* New York: Harper & Row.

Katz, Lilian. Interview by Karen Rasmussen. In "Early Childhood Education." Curriculum Update—*ASCD Newsletter* (Winter 1998): 1–8.

Lynn, Leon. 1997. "Language-Rich Home and School Environments Are Key to Reading Success." *The Harvard Education Letter* (July/August): 1–5.

Noddings, Nel. 1992. *The Challenge to Care in Schools: An Alternative Approach to Education.* New York: Teachers College Press.

Palmer, Parker J. 1998. *The Courage to Teach: Exploring the Inner Landscape of a Teacher's Life.* San Francisco: Jossey-Bass, Inc., Publishers.

Rogoff, Barbara. 1990. *Apprenticeship in Thinking: Cognitive Development in Social Context.* Oxford: Oxford University Press.

Sendak, Maurice. 1962. *Chicken Soup with Rice.* New York: HarperCollins.

Senge, Peter M., Charlotte Roberts, Richard B. Ross, Bryan J. Smith, and Art Kleiner. 1994. *The Fifth Discipline Fieldbook: Strategies and Tools for Building a Learning Organization.* New York: Currency Doubleday.

ABOUT THE AUTHOR

Roxann Kriete currently directs the Publishing branch of Northeast Foundation for Children (NEFC). She has worked at Northeast Foundation for thirteen years, teaching in NEFC's laboratory school in grades five through eight. Before that she taught high school English. She has a BA from Bucknell University.

The Responsive Classroom

To find out more about The Responsive Classroom® or to receive our free newsletter published quarterly, contact us at

NORTHEAST FOUNDATION FOR CHILDREN
71 Montague City Road, Greenfield, MA 01301
Phone: 1-800-360-6332   Fax: 413-772-2097
www.responsiveclassroom.org